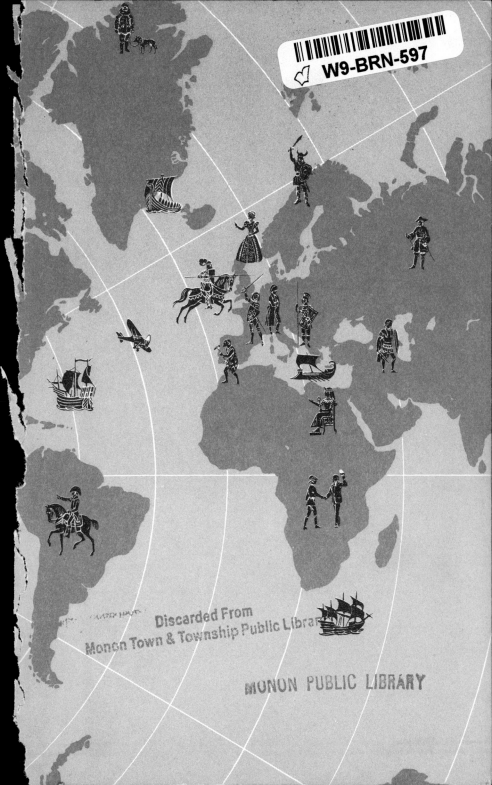

W9-BRN-597

Discarded From
Monon Town & Township Public Library

MONON PUBLIC LIBRARY

THE STORY OF ALBERT SCHWEITZER

THE STORY OF

ALBERT SCHWEITZER

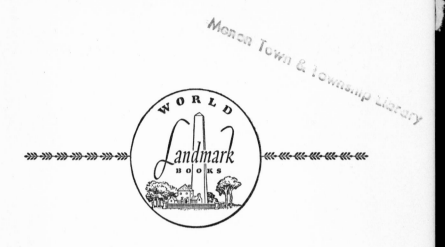

WORLD
Landmark
BOOKS

Monon Town & Township Library

BY ANITA DANIEL

Illustrated with photographs by ERICA ANDERSON
and drawings by W. T. MARS

THIS SPECIAL EDITION IS PRINTED AND DISTRIBUTED BY
ARRANGEMENT WITH THE ORIGINATORS AND PUBLISHERS
OF LANDMARK BOOKS *Random House, Inc.,* NEW YORK, BY

E. M. HALE AND COMPANY
EAU CLAIRE, WISCONSIN

© Copyright 1957, by Anita Daniel
All rights reserved under International and
Pan-American Copyright Conventions
Published in New York by Random House, Inc.
and simultaneously in Toronto, Canada, by
Random House of Canada, Limited
Library of Congress Catalog Card Number: 57-7517
Manufactured in the United States of America
by H. Wolff, New York

Contents

MONON PUBLIC LIBRARY

"*The most important years in life are those be-tween nine and fourteen. This is the time to plant the seeds of knowledge in the mind—afterwards it is too late. This is the time to ac-quaint the young with the great spirits of man-kind. . . .*"

ALBERT SCHWEITZER

THE STORY OF ALBERT SCHWEITZER

MONON PUBLIC LIBRARY

1

The Little House in the Jungle

It is night in the heart of Africa. In the jungle stands a small house. The hot wind caresses the leaves of the palm trees and brings the scent of tropical flowers. Strange sounds of wild animals are heard at frequent intervals.

At the window of the small house there is a light. Coming nearer, one can see the figure of a tall man sitting at a table. His furrowed face is crowned with thick, unruly white hair. In his powerful hand he holds a pen which he moves very slowly.

When he lifts his face from the paper, one is struck by the youthful glimmer of his eyes, by the beauty of his face. From time to time he has a tender smile for a big cat sitting on the table amongst the pile of papers.

The room is utterly simple—a bed, a chair, a few photographs, a small piano. In front of the door a fat pig is sleeping with one of her piglets.

The man at the table gets up once in a while, looks into the dark forest and affectionately at the animals, and returns to his writing. He is the only one awake at this hour and he will stay awake a great part of the night. It is the only time that belongs to him, the time when he can think about the world, about humanity, about the mysteries of eternity—and when he can dream of the music which fills his heart.

The lonely place is the famous jungle hospital of Lambaréné, French Equatorial Africa.

The man is Dr. Albert Schweitzer, one of the

greatest men of our time, and one of the greatest men of all times.

He is over eighty years old. His stature is erect, his pace is alert. From the remoteness of the African jungle his fame has spread over the whole world. Millions of people in all countries love him. His books are read in all languages. The records of his organ renditions are played everywhere.

He is world-famed as a philosopher, as a musician, as a writer, as a pioneer, and as the missionary doctor. Six hundred native families are under his personal care.

His day begins at 6:30. After breakfast, at 8 o'clock, he starts his tremendous daily work—interrupted only by lunch and half an hour of rest—and he continues till 7 o'clock at night.

He makes his rounds of the sick, the lepers, the natives afflicted with terrible tropical diseases. He removes bandages, inspects wounds, gives his advice and orders to the young doctors and the devoted nurses who form his staff. He examines hundreds of new patients who come down the river by canoe with their families. He supervises the building of huts; he lends a hand everywhere, climbing on ladders, explaining, and showing how this or that should be done. He inspects the vegetable gardens that he has planted; he watches the distribution of the food rations, seeing that each person gets his fair share.

There are always some animals with him for he loves animals dearly. Household members are Albertine, Pansy, and Sisi, the cats; Eleanor, the antelope; Tristan, Parsifal, and Lohengrin, the pelicans; Tchutchu, the dog; Lisi, the goose; Tecla and Isabel, the pigs; Poudecou, the parakeet. These animals are his joy and provide his relaxation. Their attachment warms his heart. It seems that only they never ask anything of him—and he understands their language.

His only other relaxation is music. Late at night, when he is not working on his medical charts, answering some of the thousands of weekly letters, or writing a book, he plays the piano.

And so, if you approach the Doctor's little

house at night, long before you see his bushy white head through the window you may hear the sounds of a Bach sonata or of a Beethoven symphony coming from the dark. It is a strange sensation to hear this music in the midst of the tropical jungle, accompanied sometimes by the distant howling of wild animals.

This wonderful, solitary man at the piano, this indefatigable worker has had the fullest life one can imagine. It has been overflowing with action and excitement, with tremendous adventure, with thrills. Still, he fired no guns, he killed no enemies, and his only weapons were his never-failing faith, his courage, and his love.

The story of Albert Schweitzer is the most inspiring example of what a man can achieve when he maintains the ideals of his early youth throughout his life.

2

Who Is Albert Schweitzer?

Albert Schweitzer was born on January 14, 1875, in the little village of Kaysersberg in Alsace.

Alsace—now a part of France—is a very special corner of Europe. It lies between France and Germany, to the north of Switzerland. A lovely, fertile country of hills and valleys, it is proud of its cities, for each one has long been known as a cradle of culture: Strasbourg, Metz, Colmar. Their cathedrals and museums contain priceless treasures, and many of the beautiful old houses are still inhabited by descendants of the families who built them.

But this flourishing country that breathes peace and wealth has been torn by cruel wars again and again. Both France and Germany claimed it for centuries. Following each war, Alsace went to the winner. The population was forced to transfer its allegiance from one country to the other, and from one language to the other, and to learn to obey a new ruler. Severe laws forced the Alsatians to speak, to think, to act as Germans at one time, as Frenchmen at another. In their schools the children often were forbidden to speak or to write the language they were taught at home.

In 1919, after the first World War, Alsace again became French. Its heart had always belonged to France, but because of these continual changes, perhaps also to preserve their dignity as a group over the centuries, the inhabitants developed their own special Alsatian characteristics. For example, they talk Alsatian, a language combining both French and German elements. No matter what flag flies over them, Alsatians love their country with all their soul. They are strong, confident, proud citizens who do not really resemble either the Germans or the French—and yet, they apparently have some qualities of both. They love life, laughter, food, and wine. But at the same time they work hard to earn their right to those blessings. Every Alsatian has his roots deeply set in his native soil.

Albert Schweitzer, the most famous of his countrymen, was a true child of Alsace throughout his long and exciting life. In the depths of the African jungle, where he chose to live, his mighty dreams went back to the village of his childhood. And whenever he returned to Europe, it was to Alsace that he came for a rest.

When he was born, little Albert was so tiny and weak that there seemed not much hope of keeping him alive. His mother wept as well-meaning old aunts and gossiping neighbors stood mournfully shaking their heads over the baby.

Soon after his birth the Schweitzer family moved to the village of Gunsbach. Here Albert, his brother, and his two sisters spent their happy, healthy childhood. Albert's father, Pastor Schweitzer, was the Protestant minister of the only Gunsbach church. His mother was a daughter of Pastor Schillinger. The most tolerant atmosphere pervaded this deeply religious home.

The little church—in the finest Christian spirit of brotherhood—served in turn the Protestant and the Catholic faith. Albert cherished the place. Even at a time when he was too small to understand the words, he loved to listen to his father's Sunday sermons. He saw the reverent expression on the people's faces, and he felt proud of his father for keeping them spellbound. He was enchanted with the colorful display of the Virgin and the Saints at the Catholic service. But it was the sound of the church organ that filled his heart with the greatest delight and stirred all his longings.

Albert was a dreamer. When he went to primary school, he sat gazing through the windows, wishing he were running over the hills, through the vineyards and the green meadows. It was very hard to sit still on the wooden bench and learn how to spell and how to count.

From his earliest youth he had an inquisitive mind. He could dream of meadows and hills, but when he set his mind to work it produced questions that annoyed and often bewildered his elders—questions about Jesus, about people and things around him. Where on earth did he get all those strange ideas, they wondered! One of the many problems that worried Albert was the story of Jesus and the Wise Men from the East. What did Joseph and Mary do with all the gold and the jewels that were brought to the Holy Child? How was it that Jesus and his family continued to be so poor? And it seemed incomprehensible to him that those Wise Men from the East did not continue to take care of the child Jesus.

At times Albert also acted strangely. He had grown to be a very strong and healthy boy, who loved the games of all young boys. He liked to measure his strength against the others by fighting and scuffling. Once he wrestled with a boy bigger than he, who had angered him by saying, "Come on, you fine gentleman!" indicating that the minister's son was of another class—the very thing that Albert hated most. Showing unexpected strength and ability, he got the big boy down on his knees. Resentfully the boy looked up and said, "If I ate meat twice a week like you do, I'd be just as strong—see!"

Albert was deeply shocked; it confirmed him in the belief that he was "different" from his schoolmates. As the minister's son he lived on a higher level than the other boys. He was conscious of this advantage and he felt hurt by it. He would not be an object of envy. He would not wear better clothes. He was so stubborn about it that his mother finally had to give in and permit her son to wear old slacks, "sabots," (wooden shoes), a weatherworn cap—the kind of clothes worn by the other village children. His stern refusal to wear an overcoat to church on cold winter Sundays forced his father to box his ears. But despite this punishment, his father understood the boy's inner reasons: Albert would not wear his overcoat because the other boys had none.

Outwardly then, he was like the other boys: he wore the same clothes and played the same games. But inwardly he was different. He had a very strong sense of right and wrong; and when he had done wrong, he suffered intensely. He soon learned to keep his thoughts to himself for fear the other boys would think him a "sissy." For example, from his earliest childhood he had always loved animals so dearly that he included them in his daily prayers. When he had hurt a dog or a horse by accident or by thoughtlessness, he felt wretched for weeks.

One day, when he was seven years old, his friends came to fetch him; they were all going bird-shooting. Most reluctantly, but wanting to be a good sport, Albert went along. The boys crept up to a tree, slings in hand. The birds were singing gaily. At this very moment—it was exactly noon—the church bells began to peal.

It was like a sign from Heaven, a divine reminder: "Albert, *thou* shalt not kill. . . ."

Albert dropped his gun. He shouted to frighten off the birds and he fled, tears of shame and relief running down his cheeks. From this moment on, his mind was made up: never, never would he kill for the thrill of killing.

It was the starting point of his "reverence for life," which later was to become the essence of his philosophy and an inspiration to millions of people all over the world.

At Colmar, the nearest big city to the village of Gunsbach, Albert had his first glimpse of a Negro and he was deeply impressed. This was not a live Negro, but one of several stone figures of a large monument which stood on a public square. It was the work of the famous French sculptor, Bartoldi, who also made the Statue of Liberty, the symbol of New York harbor. The beautiful and sad expression on the huge Negro's face touched Albert's sensitive heart in such a way that from then on, whenever he was in Colmar, he never failed to visit this statue. Later, much later, when he was spending most of his time among the dark-skinned population in Africa, he often recalled how fate had given him a hint of his future life when he was still a little boy.

Colmar evokes another childhood remembrance: This ancient city has a lovely museum containing unique treasures, among which are the famous altar paintings by Matthias Grunewald. They present a very realistic picture of the birth and the life of Christ. Albert was immensely impressed to see that Christ and his apostles had lived in much the same way as he did. The simple utensils he saw in the pictures were the same that were used in his own home; it brought Christ still closer to him.

But what pleased him most of all was St. John's thick mop of disorderly hair. Albert had always suffered on account of his unruly hair, which his mother insisted had to be brushed with hard strokes and groomed with oil to give the boy a neater appearance. How often had he heard his parents say, "Disorderly hair is proof of a disorderly character," and "Undisciplined hair shows lack of inner discipline." Here in the picture was a confirmed saint, with exactly the same rebellious hair! At once his heart filled with pity, for he knew what St. John must have suffered. But then he thought that if despite his hair John had become a saint, then it did not matter what one's hair looked like. From that time on, Albert lost his feelings of guilt, brought about by the well-intentioned but rather silly exhortations which had made him suffer so much.

These little childhood events remained forever vivid in Albert Schweitzer's memory. He often repeated, as a grown-up man, that adults greatly underestimate the sensitivity of a child.

In spite of these little problems, Albert was extremely happy at home. His mother was never a great talker and she was rather strict, but though she was not demonstrative, Albert could feel her warmth and tenderness. Indeed, she dearly loved her son Albert, the boy who was so different from the others. His father was the kindest and most natural of men. Albert loved him very much. At a time when parents were more feared than loved, Albert's father seemed a great exception. He always had time for his children, and made them welcome in his rather awe-inspiring study which was filled with books from the floor to the ceiling.

There was only one thing about his father that caused Albert to despair. This was his insistence that his children write long, detailed "thank-you" letters for every little Christmas or birthday gift they received. On this point he was inexorable; the children must come to his study and show him every single letter before it could be mailed. All the joy of getting presents was spoiled by the dreaded ordeal of writing these letters! Remembering this all his life, he never sent any child a gift without a note stating that he did not want any "thank-you" letter.

At the age of nine, Albert started going to school in Munster. It was over two miles to the little town and Albert loved these daily walks, particularly when he could take them alone. He delighted in watching the coming of each new season, the birds, the flowers, the insects.

The countryside was lovely, and the boy had a great feeling for nature. Nothing escaped his attention and he liked to be alone with his thoughts.

From the earliest days Albert Schweitzer was profoundly concerned with the suffering he saw around him. Why was there so much suffering among men and animals, and what could one do to relieve it? He himself lacked nothing—he was strong, healthy, and happy. But he never took these things for granted—quite the contrary. Deep in his heart grew the belief that was to become the guiding light of his life: those who are blessed with happiness shall pay for it by dedicating themselves to the underprivileged who do not enjoy such blessings.

He was a better student now, but by no means a model one. He loved to laugh and he laughed easily. His schoolmates knew this and did their best to arouse his merriment in the classroom. This never failed to anger his teachers; laughing in class was considered bad behavior. In his school reports again and again appeared the remark: "Schweitzer laughs too much."

Still, he had an earnest and even solemn nature. Later, he often used to say that he inherited from his mother both the reluctance to show his feelings and a strong temper. He was as passionate in his games as in everything he did. One day he struck his sister Louise because she did not take the game they were playing as seriously as he did. After this he became afraid of his violent disposition and gradually gave up playing games.

As far back as he could remember, music always had been the dream and the delight of his life. When he was only five, his father gave him his first piano lessons. Soon after that he was permitted to start playing the organ, for which he showed an amazing aptitude from the start. At nine, when his legs were barely long enough to reach the pedals, he began replacing the organist in his father's church.

His passion for this instrument was so tremendous that he dreamed of one day becoming a great musician.

The Alsace of Albert's childhood was under German domination, and his education followed the strict German system and discipline. When the time came for him to go to the "Gymnasium" or High School, he was sent to Mulhouse, a city near the Swiss border, to live with his Uncle Louis and Aunt Sophie. They were a fine, elderly, childless couple who had offered to take care of Albert during his high-school years and to pay for his studies. Albert's father, whose salary was meager indeed, could not have afforded this by himself.

Aunt Sophie ruled her house with a stern hand and no fun was allowed. Albert greatly missed the gay, warm atmosphere of his parents' home, the company of his brother and sisters, and perhaps most of all the loveliness of the countryside and his carefree outdoor life. His days now were filled with work—there was no time left for strolls in the fields and no more time for dreaming. But even though he was often homesick, the sensitive boy knew that his relatives meant well.

All his life Albert Schweitzer remained sincerely grateful to his aunt, who had compelled him to practice the piano so many hours every day. But oh, how he hated to stay indoors and practice scales when outside the sun was shining!

In his new school in Mulhouse, Albert met a very fine teacher, who inspired him with self-confidence and was the first to develop in him a passion for learning. Albert found languages and mathematics very hard—but he soon discovered the fascination of mastering those subjects for which he had neither inclination nor talent. It became a kind of sport to take on the hardest things and to overcome the difficulties.

He became a passionate reader. He read voraciously all the books he could lay his hands on. His Aunt Sophie, a former schoolteacher, was appalled at the speed with which he read classics, scientific and religious books, and piles of newspapers. Here she drew the line: newspapers she would not tolerate. They were full of crimes and love stories. "Yes, Aunt Sophie,"

Albert protested, "but what I'm interested in is politics!"

"Let me ask him a few questions," suggested Uncle Louis. He asked Albert the names of the princes of Greece, the subject of the latest speech at the Reichstag, the names of the ministers of the French government—in other words, the front-page news of the time.

Albert knew all the answers. Uncle Louis was dumfounded. Why, the boy absorbed reading as a sponge absorbs water! From then on, Albert was allowed to read whatever he pleased. And Uncle Louis made a habit of discussing current events with his nephew.

In his old age Albert Schweitzer said many times that the most important years of one's life are between nine and fourteen. This, he said, was when the brain was most receptive, and when boys and girls should be introduced to the great ideas of the best thinkers of all times.

Next to his school work and reading, music took a great place in Albert's daily schedule. He had the good fortune to become the pupil of the famous organist Eugene Münch, who greatly contributed to developing the boy's musical ability.

The long school years passed, and all too soon Albert Schweitzer faced the graduation examinations. Under the German rule this was a real ordeal. The boys, attired in stiff, black frock coats, appeared in turn in front of the assembled faculty for individual questioning. It was a nightmare!

Albert did not have a black outfit and, since it was expensive, he did not want to buy one. So he borrowed a coat and a pair of black trousers from his uncle, who was a good deal shorter than himself. With a piece of string tied to his suspenders he lowered the pants to the level of his ankles. There was nothing he could do about the fit of the coat and the sleeves that were too short. Long, lean Albert cut a very funny figure. His appearance provoked fits of uncontrollable laughter among his fellow students and the whole assembly. The dean was outraged. How dared this student make fun of the solemn procedure? Viciously he tormented

Albert with the most difficult questions in mathematics. No doubt Albert would have failed, had not history followed. On this subject he was so outstanding that the questioning professor, himself an erudite historian, was thrilled by the brilliant answers.

Thanks to his knowledge of history and in spite of his hilarious appearance in his uncle's short and baggy trousers, Albert passed his final examinations and was graduated from the Gymnasium.

Albert was eighteen and burning to go to Paris. His aim and secret hope were to become the pupil of the most famous organ-player, Charles Louis Widor. Now his dream came true and, arriving in Paris, he presented himself with a great deal of trepidation. He need not have worried. Struck by the amazing talent of this young, shy Alsatian boy, the musician decided to make an artist of him. He never had a more enthusiastic and devoted pupil. From now on, Albert was a very busy young man. He divided his time between Strasbourg, where he studied theology and philosophy at the University, and Paris, where he worked with Widor.

Within a few months, however, his studies were interrupted by military service. For a whole year Albert dutifully goose-stepped and maneuvered with the German army. But the life of a soldier was not to the taste of a young man whose mind was filled with ideals of a very different kind. Making the best of a bad situation, he trained himself to lead two separate lives: one was physical drudgery and the other intellectual delight.

During the day, like a good soldier, he carried out his orders. But while he marched, scrubbed the floor, or peeled potatoes, he was preparing in his mind a book on the life of Jesus. At night when others slept, he studied Greek.

After discharging his duties toward the state, Albert returned to his studies. He worked passionately. He never accepted what he read, even when it was written by men of genius whom he profoundly admired, until he understood it. As a small boy he had often angered his elders by plying them with questions about things everybody took for granted. Now that he was a young man, he stopped asking others. Instead, he tried to find the answers within himself. One may say without any fear of exaggeration that there was not a single moment in Albert Schweitzer's life when his mind was not active. He admitted that he was a dreamer. But this extraordinary dreamer never lost the sense of reality and he succeeded in making many of his dreams come true. Still, nothing in his career came easily. Whatever he accomplished was due to unceasing efforts of mind and will and to many hours of solitary thought.

Solitary thought was somewhat easier in Schweitzer's youth than it is today. At that time there were no radios, no television sets, and none of the many other distracting inventions which surround us today. The automobile was a brand-new invention available only to a wealthy few. The great fad of the 1890s was the bicycle. It was considered a luxury and frowned upon by the grownups who said it made young people too independent! With his first savings Albert bought one—and enjoyed it immensely. Many people considered it indecent for a minister's son, himself a student of theology, to ride this way, and criticized him. Albert was never bothered by such comments. His conscience was much more severe in judging his own acts than anything that others could say. He went on bicycling.

After passing his theological examinations, Albert moved to Paris. This gave him more time for organ-playing. Here he continued his philosophical studies at the old and famous university—the Sorbonne. He wrote a book about the philosophy of Kant. And he continued to work on his thesis for a doctorate in theology. In 1899, he was appointed to serve at the Saint Nicholas Church of Strasbourg. A year later, after he had been ordained, he was made a curate.

Among the curate's duties was preaching. Albert Schweitzer prepared his sermons very conscientiously and often rewrote them as many as three times. Still the churchgoers found cause for complaint: the sermons were much too short! Albert Schweitzer was told to make them longer. He begged his superior to explain to the congregation that he was still a very young man without much experience. He simply had to stop speaking when he felt he had nothing more to say! Even so, he had to promise that he would try to make his sermons last at least twenty minutes.

3

The Great Decision

One day, while vacationing in his beloved
Gunsbach, Albert Schweitzer made the greatest decision of his life.

It was a radiant June day. The sky was blue.
The trees were in flower. The church bells
were gaily pealing. The world was incredibly
beautiful. Albert felt all this with an emotion so
deep that it almost caused physical pain.

Climbing the familiar path through the woods, he searched himself with innermost concentration: "How is it possible that I, Albert Schweitzer, should enjoy such health, such a happy home, a beautiful country, a brilliant career—while all over the world there is such terrible suffering, so much injustice? Can I accept all these blessings as a gift? As my birthright?"

"No," said an inner voice, "you cannot."

"What must I do?"

"You must pay for the blessings you have received and for all the gifts that are yours—you must give of yourself. . . ."

Now Albert Schweitzer clearly saw before him the road he was going to follow throughout his life.

And he took a sacred vow: he would continue to study theology, philosophy and music until he was thirty years old. But from then on, to the end of his days, he would devote himself entirely to the service of suffering mankind. He would follow the teachings of Jesus.

He felt utterly relieved. He had found his

goal. He would also find a way of reaching it.

He had a deadline: his 30th birthday. Nine more years to live as he pleased, doing the things he loved—studying, playing the organ, writing. There was no time to lose; he plunged into work. He passed examination after examination, got degrees and more degrees. He became a doctor of theology and a doctor of philosophy. He preached and taught, he played the organ, and he wrote.

In 1903 he was appointed principal of the Theological Seminary of Strasbourg. In 1905 his book on the life of Johann Sebastian Bach was published and acclaimed as the most outstanding study of the great composer. It made the name of Albert Schweitzer internationally known. This amazing young man deeply impressed the greatest minds of his time. He was invited to play the organ and to lecture in England, in Sweden, in Germany, in France.

Every vacation and holiday he spent at the parsonage of Gunsbach. It was good to be close to the earth. And the warmth of his paternal home delighted him.

MONON PUBLIC LIBRARY

Years passed. One more year and he would be thirty. And still he had no idea how to fulfill his sacred vow.

He had thought of all kinds of ways he could serve mankind. There were orphans and abandoned children one could educate, neglected children to care for. He could devote himself to tramps, or look after discharged prisoners. . . .

But all such work required constant coöperation with welfare organizations. Albert Schweitzer wanted no committee meetings, no membership in any organization. Deep within him was the urge to work in direct contact with those who suffered and were in need of help. But he must be completely free to do it in his own way.

Then, suddenly, he found the answer.

"One morning in the autumn of 1904 I found on my writing table in the college one of the green-covered magazines in which the Paris Missionary Society reported every month on its activities. I mechanically opened the magazine which had been laid on my table during my absence. As I did so, my eye caught the title of an article: 'The Needs of the Congo Mission.' It was by Alfred Boegner, the President of the Paris Missionary Society, an Alsatian, and it contained a complaint that the mission had not enough workers to carry on its work in the Gabon, the northern province of the Congo Colony. The writer expressed his hope that this appeal would bring some of those 'on whom the Master's eye had already rested,' to a decision to offer themselves for this urgent work. The conclusion said, 'Men and women who can simply reply to the Master's call, "Lord, I am coming," those are the people whom the Church needs.' Having finished the article, I quietly began my work. My search was over."

Albert Schweitzer spent his 30th birthday in solitary contemplation and self-examination. He considered his plan from every point of view; so great a venture could not be undertaken without a careful examination of one's assets. Health, great energy, practical sense he had. He was tough and prudent. He knew he had very few wants. He was sure he could face disappointments and even failure. And in his heart he felt that he was on the right way.

Yes, he was able to carry out this plan.

And so he sat down and wrote six letters to his family and to his closest friends, quietly informing them that he had chosen to lead the life of a missionary in the African jungle. He went down the street and dropped the letters in a mailbox.

A storm of protest followed. Had the young man gone out of his mind? How could he take such a momentous decision from one day to another? It simply could not be true. No one, of course, had known of his vow of many years before, or indeed of the many inner struggles that he had to overcome before he came to this decision.

When his friends and family perceived his inflexible will, there started a real campaign to dissuade him from this folly. How could a man of such promise give up his career just as he was starting it? His music teachers were heartbroken to see this brilliant artist abandon music. His family tried to show him how he could serve humanity by remaining where he was, without giving up anything. Poor Albert Schweitzer passed through a terrible time. No one seemed to understand that he had to do what he was doing—that is, with one exception.

This was a young woman called Helene Bresslau. She was the daughter of a great scholar and an ardent student of philosophy. She and Albert had known each other for a number of years. They had many common interests; they shared many views. These they used to discuss sitting on a bench of the university, or walking in the country.

Helene was the only person to whom Albert could speak of the questions that were burning in his heart. She listened quietly and he knew that she understood him. Now, at this fateful moment of his life, when everyone around him showed not the slightest comprehension of what he wanted to do, only Helene Bresslau stood by his side.

With sadness Albert Schweitzer realized that

even many of the good Christians only talked
about Christian principles. What he wanted to
do was to put these principles into action.

Actually he now took a step that made his
well-wishers feel even worse: before he went
to Africa, he decided that he must first become a
physician.

Why did he need to study medicine? Had he
not studied enough?

Albert Schweitzer had read about the terrible tropical diseases and the lack of medical
help. He was profoundly shocked. People in Africa were dying when they could have been
saved—if a physician had been there to take care
of them. Was it not the duty of the white man
to share the blessings of progress in medicine
with his underprivileged brother?

He wanted to help the Negroes, cure their
ills and show them the way to better health and
better living. A missionary was not enough. He
must have a medical degree, even if this meant
postponing his plan.

And so, at the age of thirty, this doctor of

philosophy and doctor of theology, an accomplished organist, and famous writer, went back to school as a student of medicine.

The years that followed the great decision were perhaps the most strenuous years in Albert Schweitzer's life. He did not give up his preaching, nor abandon the boys he was preparing for confirmation. He went on with his music recitals. He continued his writing, particularly on a subject that was very close to his heart: the life of Jesus. All this while he was a student at medical school. Luckily he had trained himself to enjoy things best when they came hardest.

Studying medicine all day and writing almost all night, he was often utterly exhausted. But he never lost his good spirits. His lectures and his concerts brought him the money to pay for his studies. And as he pursued his work on the life of Jesus, he became more and more convinced that he was on the right road.

How, with all this, he could take on still another task is impossible to imagine, and yet that is what he did. From his earliest childhood, organs had always entranced him. It was from his maternal grandfather Schillinger that he must have inherited his passion for this instrument. He was ever fond of recalling how his grandfather—a famous organ player and organ builder—always gave a little speech to his workers before they started working on a new organ: "You will be well paid and well fed—but beware! Heaven forbid that I discover any one of you working too fast! Take your time; you must work as slowly as you can . . ."

Each time Albert Schweitzer told this story he laughed: "And today we urge everybody to make everything as quickly as possible!"

Whatever the reason, these old slowly-built organs had, according to some—including Albert—a much richer and warmer tone than the new electric organs. Others disagreed. Soon arguments were flying back and forth.

Albert Schweitzer threw himself into the controversy. But instead of arguing, he sat down and wrote a pamphlet on the art of organ-building and organ-playing. Within a short time of its publication, he was proclaimed the greatest authority on the subject by all—except the builders of mechanized organs, who became his enemies. But this sort of thing never stopped Albert Schweitzer from speaking the truth.

His faith and idealism, added to his natural physical strength, gave him unbelievable energy. But he was the first to admit, years later, that his period of medical studies was the most exhausting of his life.

After six years of medicine Albert Schweitzer passed his final examination in 1911. He paid the fee for it with money he had earned playing the organ at a music festival.

To become a full-fledged physician, he still had to serve as an interne in a hospital. During that year he married Helene Bresslau who, in the meantime, had become a trained nurse so that she could assist him in his medical work.

The young couple spent a last badly needed vacation in the parsonage at Gunsbach, where Albert, never inactive, revised his "Historical Jesus."

They were ready to leave when a new complication arose. Albert Schweitzer had received his credentials from the Paris Missionary Society to do medical work in French Equatorial Africa. He had also received a grant for a few acres of land to build a hospital there. But, of course—no funds. Before he could leave, Albert Schweitzer had to raise money. He had to ask people to support something as yet existing solely in his own mind—a mere project based on good will, on hope, and on personal courage. It was no easy task. But nothing had ever come the easy way in Albert Schweitzer's life.

Thanks to devoted friends and admirers, and thanks also to the royalties earned by his books, he succeeded in gathering the money. For some of it he bought gold, which he carefully sewed into a linen bag. To his astonished wife he said: "One must be prepared for everything—some day there might be a war."

And now he set out for his new goal—Africa.

In order to understand the human greatness of Albert Schweitzer's decision, it is necessary to recall again and again how deeply he had loved every single phase of his work and studies. He had a passion for music, philosophy, theology. For him preaching was a joy and so was learning or discussing great ideas with the great thinkers of his time. He was profoundly attached to his family, to his church, to his friends, and he had never felt happier than in his Alsatian home at Gunsbach.

It was a superhuman effort to part with all these things he so passionately loved—to start a new life on a strange continent of which he knew only its misery, ignorance, and deadly dangers.

With all the world shaking its head at his folly, with his own heart at the breaking point, he never faltered. Albert Schweitzer's inner voice was stronger than all the voices around him. And it was this voice that he was ready to follow.

4
Trials

And so, on a glorious Good Friday of the year 1913, Albert Schweitzer, accompanied by his wife, left Europe and all he knew behind him and soon sailed for the Africa he knew only from books and from hearsay.

With seventy boxes of medicines and surgical instruments, equipped with unshakable faith and tremendous good will, he began his long voyage into the unknown.

He was going on his own, as a doctor, without any responsibility to any committee or organization. He had received permission from the Paris Missionary Society to build his hospital on a few acres the Society owned on the Ogowe River in French Equatorial Africa. But he had to promise them that he would remain mute as a fish in matters of theology. The Society did not quite trust the temperamental young man to conform completely with their rules. Outside of this one binding promise, he was his own master. So started the greatest adventure of his life.

The Schweitzers sailed from Bordeaux, on the west coast of France. Their fellow passengers were French soldiers on their way to join their African regiments, French colonial employees, and various officials—people who had lived in Africa for years and were returning there after a vacation in their homeland.

Eager to learn as much as possible about the continent where he was going to live, Schweitzer encouraged them to talk. What he heard saddened him but confirmed the necessity of what he had set out to do. For all these good people were totally resigned to the misery, sickness, and ignorance of the natives. They were fully aware that by bringing them liquor, the white man had worsened their condition. And yet, they did nothing to bring about a change for the better. The missionaries, of course, had tried their best to help. However, their efforts were necessarily limited to caring for the natives' sick souls. But what about the sick bodies? What Africa needed was doctors, doctors, and more doctors! This was the reason why Schweitzer had studied medicine before going to Africa. Now he could hardly wait to reach his destination and start his work. Although he never quite realized the colossal difficulties that awaited him, he fortunately was fully equipped for the hard struggle ahead.

The crossing lasted several weeks and the weather was very stormy. Most of the passengers were seasick. But not Schweitzer. Having met a specialist in tropical medicine aboard, he spent

MONON PUBLIC LIBRARY

hours every day in discussion with him. It was from this doctor that he accidentally received his first warning: "Never, never take one step in Africa without a tropical helmet on your head." For if a white man exposed his bare head to the sun for even a few minutes he might become delirious. Only the natives were safe, with their heads protected by thick black hair, and their bodies shielded by the dark pigment of their skin.

While almost everyone on board was worn out by the long and uncomfortable trip, Albert Schweitzer was full of joy and excitement when the ship finally weighed anchor at Libreville.

As the small white steamer, which they had boarded at Cape Lopez, slowly wound its way up the broad Ogowe River, the Schweitzers had their first taste of the almost unbearable tropical heat and felt the fierce bites of the African mosquitoes. The first impressions were overwhelming. Sluggish yellow waters flowed between two impenetrable walls of the primeval forest. Here and there the dark foliage of the jungle was aflame with the bright flowers of lianas, green and red parrots, crested cranes, weaverbirds, kingfishers, flashy gold and green pippios and round-eyed owls. Birds of every color and shape were flying, singing, and fishing under the eyes of the excited voyagers. Gorgeously colored butterflies fluttered in the still air. And there—the first monkeys! They stared at the Schweitzers from the palm trees, while from the muddy banks crocodiles sleepily blinked at the familiar sight of the paddlewheeler.

But it was not unalloyed beauty. In the terrible heat, clothes were wet, bodies felt slimy.

At sundown the steamer anchored in a small bay, leaving again at dawn on the last leg of the journey. As the river narrowed, the current became stronger and it took another day before the Schweitzers finally had the first glimpse of their destination: Lambaréné.

Lambaréné lies on a narrow island amid the waters of the Ogowe River. Long before Albert Schweitzer made it famous all around the world it had already found its place in the history

books of French children. It was from here
that, in 1875, the Frenchman Savorgnan de
Brazza started on his voyage of exploration for
the source of the Ogowe River.

Slave trade was still flourishing, though already the English and the French were hunting
slave traders all along the West African coast.
Wherever they caught a transport they liberated
the slaves, who later settled at a spot named
"Libreville," which in French means "free
city."

Whenever Savorgnan de Brazza met the sad
lines of hapless Negroes being led into slavery,
he bought them and freed them. Thus he made
friends with the chiefs, who called him "pro-
tector of the natives," and he was able to con-
quer a vast territory for France without blood-
shed.

Actually, the first colonists to come to Lambaréné were Americans who arrived some
twenty years earlier, in the 1850s. They built
their house upon a little hill commanding a
good view of all approaches, which made them

feel somewhat safer in a country inhabited by cannibals.

When, thanks to de Brazza, the territory known as the Gabon became French, the Paris Missionary Society took over the post. It was on these grounds that Albert Schweitzer was to build his hospital.

Lambaréné was an ideal spot for this purpose. The Ogowe River, with its hundreds of miles of waterways reaching far into the jungle, was most convenient for the natives traveling in their canoes. Besides, there was not a single physician within a hundred miles.

But this ideal spot in 1913 had no decent landing place. So the Schweitzers were forced to abandon their steamer and transfer once more, this time to native canoes made of hollow tree trunks. These were long, very narrow and very delicately balanced conveyances which required in their handling a great deal of skill and on the part of the Schweitzers a great deal of confidence. But courageously they let themselves down, and holding fast to the sides of the canoe, they completed the last lap of their long, long journey.

It was a gay trip. The young paddlers sang merry native songs all along the way, while they paddled, standing up, keeping their canoes in balance with their bodies.

White mission people, black people, and swarms of black children, all wanting to help unload the luggage, greeted the Schweitzers upon landing.

They were home at last!

But it soon appeared that it was not much of a home. Inspecting the small house with the aid of a kerosene lamp, the Schweitzers saw to their horror a room full of flying cockroaches and an enormous spider—so disgusting that impulsively Schweitzer killed it. It was the first and probably the last time he ever killed a spider. This repulsive insect, he soon learned, was very useful since it fed on the malaria-bearing mosquito.

The house stood high above the ground on iron pillars. It was surrounded by a porch. Through the window the view was wonderful.

But inside, there was nothing to look at, just two small, bare rooms.

Schweitzer cared little how he was housed, at least in the beginning. But where, where was there even a crude structure which he could use to start the hospital?

The lumbering season was in full swing, explained the missionaries who had welcomed him. All hands were busy cutting mahogany, rosewood, and other fine wood for export. It was impossible to build without help.

Where, then, would he store his seventy precious cases of medical supplies, the arrival of which he expected within a week or two?

Above all, what was he to do with all these people? Surrounding Schweitzer was a crowd of men, women, and children. Their coal-black eyes were fixed upon him, silently, ardently, pleading.

The word had spread far and wide that a doctor was coming and nothing would stop the natives from journeying to Lambaréné. Canoes loaded with the sick and their families continued to arrive. The sick painfully climbed up from the river, or were carried up to Schweitzer's little house on the hill by their relatives. He must look after them—but how, and where . . . ?

Right from the start, from the moment he set foot in Lambaréné, Albert Schweitzer faced the simple, yet overwhelming and ever present fact: whatever it was he wanted, he had to do himself.

Some natives had contagious diseases. Fearing others might catch them, he would not allow the sick into the two little rooms of his house. So he started practicing in the open air. Drenched with sweat, he worked under the torrid African sun. Regularly every evening thunderstorms came. Rain poured down in sheets. All the supplies had to be rushed under the porch.

At night, Schweitzer tumbled into his bed, exhausted, but unable to fall asleep. He lay awake for hours, worrying about his patients. If he had the necessary drugs and installations, he could save so many of them. And when the boxes with medicine arrived, workers were still unavailable.

He would have to find some other way of providing a roof over his head when he was operating. Searching the hospital grounds, he discovered an empty chicken house—long in disuse, since its inhabitants had been attacked and devoured alive by armies of traveling ants. Why not use it?

The necessary repairs were soon made. The Schweitzers patched the holes in the roof as best they could. With brooms and brushes they scrubbed and whitewashed the walls. A cot borrowed from the mission house was placed in the center of the floor and served as an operating table.

In this tiny, windowless room the heat was atrocious. To make matters worse, the thatched roof let the dangerous sun rays come through. So both the Doctor and the nurse, his wife, dared not take off their heavy helmets.

No sooner had Albert Schweitzer found this temporary and uncomfortable solution than he was faced with the next problem. Every tribe spoke a different language. The small and ugly *Fanos* and the *Galloas* (who, by the way, were enemy brothers and had to be kept apart on the hospital grounds) had their own languages. There were the good-looking Simbas from the upper Ogowe, who spoke a different tongue. From the south came the *Eschisas* and the *Kouloumatous*. How was he to understand them all and how could he be understood?

A lucky discovery brought the answer. Among a batch of new patients one day arrived a bright-looking native by the name of Joseph Azvavanu, who spoke French fluently. He had been working as a cook for European settlers but had lost his job because of ill health. Schweitzer easily persuaded Joseph to remain at Lambaréné as assistant-interpreter.

Joseph was both bright and very able. He had an incredible memory. In no time he had learned to recognize the various medicines by the shape of the characters on their labels—though he continued to be unable to read them! To his new job the medical assistant brought a colorful touch. His anatomic descriptions were expressed in the language of his former culinary job. He would say, "This man has pains in his right leg of mutton." Or, "This woman has pains in her upper left cutlet and in her filet."

Medical consultations started at 8:30 in the morning. The patients sat waiting for the Doctor on shaded benches in front of the chicken house. Every morning Joseph recited the Doctor's orders in the two main idioms:

1. The Doctor forbids you to spit on the hospital grounds.
2. The Doctor forbids you to talk in a loud voice.
3. The Doctor cannot take care of everybody during the morning. So the sick and those who accompany them must bring food for one day.

Joseph ended by requesting that the words of the Doctor be spread to all the neighboring villages. After each sentence the natives shook their heads in acknowledgment. And when Joseph had finished, they commented endlessly upon the meaning of every word.

Some sort of hospital organization slowly started to emerge. The Doctor's invaluable aide, Mrs. Schweitzer, took care of the instruments and assisted with all the surgical cases. She distributed the food; she supervised the washing of the linen and the bandages. Nothing in Lambaréné was ever thrown away; bandages were washed, disinfected, and used over and over again.

Before leaving the hospital, every patient was carefully labeled. A piece of cardboard was hung around his neck, on which were inscribed his name and the number corresponding to the case history in the Doctor's book. In this book, against the patient's name, the thrifty Doctor listed not only his diagnosis and prescriptions, but also every little glass bottle or tin box in which the medicine was supplied. How precious were these things thousands of miles away from civilization, no one can imagine unless he has himself lived in the middle of the jungle. It was of the utmost importance that every one of these receptacles was returned to the hospital. Only glass or tin protected the medicine—pill, powder, liquid, or cream—against the pervading tropical humidity.

But it was a hopeless task to try to recover those precious vials—the natives found them much to their taste and wore them as ornaments —so much so, that in every one of his letters, Schweitzer implored his friends in Europe to send him empty bottles, corks, tubes, and tin containers.

At each and every step were difficulties which no one in Europe could have understood, and which Schweitzer, himself, with all his foresight, could never have imagined. Take, for instance, the matter of prescriptions—how to use the medicine that was packed in the precious bottle. It took a great deal of time and patience to teach the natives that the box or bottle carried a label which told the exact amount of medicine to be taken. Those who could read were asked to help the others. Before the patient was dismissed, Schweitzer rehearsed the prescription: "Three drops in the morning and three drops in the evening." But more likely than not, once away, the patient swallowed the

entire contents of the bottle at one gulp; ate the
pommade instead of rubbing it into his skin;
and spread the powder given him to swallow
over his ulcerated wounds. It was hopeless!

They came with every imaginable kind of
disease: malaria, dysentery, elephantiasis, lep-
rosy, skin diseases of every description, and also
terrible wounds, which often spread a pestifer-
ous odor. Men were brought in whose flesh had
been torn by leopards, crocodiles, or gorillas;
whose bodies had been trampled by elephants.
In their festering wounds were hundreds of flies
and poisonous ants.

At times Schweitzer fell into deep despair:
would he be able to cope with his self-imposed
task, with no coöperation from anywhere? His
supplies of medicine and money were soon coming to an end. The heat wore him down; the
lack of facilities sapped his strength. What
could one man do in the face of such misery?

"Yet what are all these disagreeable things
compared with the joy of being here, working,
helping?" he wrote during this same period.

MONON PUBLIC LIBRARY

"However limited one's means, how much one can do! Just to see the relief and joy of those who have been treated, bandaged, and given rest after they have dragged their poor, bleeding feet through the jungle, that in itself makes work here worthwhile."

But the physical difficulties, overwhelming as they were, were dwarfed by the superstitions, the prejudice, and the ignorance Schweitzer dealt with day after day.

The natives called the Doctor "Oganga," meaning "fetishman" or sorcerer. They were convinced that sickness was caused by evil spirits, by witchcraft, and by "the worm." They always talked about the worm. The worm had entered the feet, then it went up to the stomach or to the head. The worm was pain.

"Please, please, Oganga, drive the worm out," they begged and screamed. The worm, in many cases, was caused by a strangulated hernia as it was with Schweitzer's first surgical case, a man brought to him moaning with pain. "When you wake up, you will feel no more pain," Schweitzer said, gently caressing the bushy head. After the operation the native woke up, crying again and again, "I've no more pain! I've no more pain!" The worm had been driven from the body.

"The Doctor kills a man, then he brings him to life again," was the way the natives explained anesthesia. To Schweitzer's amazement, they all wanted to be operated on—and resented it when it was not necessary!

But it was not always so easy. Whenever a patient died because his case was hopeless, rumor had it that the white man had killed him. There was a girl who used to shriek each time she met the Doctor, "I saw with my own eyes how a living man was brought here. The Doctor stayed alone with him the whole night and the next day he was dead." Some said that he must be a "white leopardman," the most dreaded kind of man among the natives.

Leopardmen were men who believed themselves to be leopards. They ran on all fours, like leopards. They attacked their victims with leopard claws tied to their hands and feet.

Membership was by initiation only. Before becoming a member of this dreadful clan, the applicant had to drink the magic potion—human blood out of a human skull. From then on, he was bound to lead the life of a leopard, and to begin with, he had to kill a member of his family. The spell was such and the terror of reprisal so great, that no leopardman ever dared to protest against this ritual.

The French government pursued the leopardmen for years and succeeded in breaking their gruesome power by almost exterminating them.

To call the kindhearted Doctor a white leopardman, because an incurably sick man, whom he had lovingly nursed all through the night, had died in the morning only showed how fearful was the black man of the white man's "magic."

5

... and Tribulations

From near and far the natives arrived in ever growing numbers, and among the sick were many lunatics in the last stages of insanity. There was nothing that Schweitzer could do to save these poor people. But he gave a great deal of thought to the fear and the terror that could drive sane men to madness.

The terrors of the jungle were not only the

wild beasts, the tropical diseases that wasted the body, the physical pain. With the aid of modern medicine Schweitzer could bring a measure of relief to those suffering from pain. He was able to drive "the worm" from the body by extracting a diseased appendix or an infected tooth, or by sewing up a lacerated arm. But as deadly as the wild beasts and the sicknesses, were the terrible fears provoked by taboos and curses and kept alive by the all-powerful fetishmen or witch doctors.

A taboo is a religious "don't"; a sacred interdiction imposed upon an individual by a priest or witch doctor. There were taboos that applied to everybody; others were personal. For instance, it was taboo for one man to fill a hole in the earth, for another to step over a procession of ants. A woman might be forbidden to touch a broom. It might be taboo for a man to count his fingers. A boy might live all his life with the fear that someone some day would tap him on the shoulder. Twins were never to look at a rainbow. The people believed in these taboos so completely that if, by some mischance, any of these things happened to them, they became mad or died. Many such instances were witnessed by Schweitzer, who stood by helplessly—unable to prevent the tragedy.

The witch doctor played upon these fears and superstitions to his own advantage. He could never be "wrong." When need arose to show his "infallible" power, he did not hesitate to use poison to make a sick man sicker in order to perform the miracle of a cure. All must obey his every whim and order. The punishment for disobeying the witch doctor was death by poison.

Schweitzer wished he could free the natives from these fears. But how? How could he break down these superstitions based on age-old traditions and the power of the evil spirits? Patience, understanding, love, and faith were the only ways to success; he knew it. Luckily the good Doctor was well equipped with those moral weapons. Even though he was unable to speak the native languages, there emanated from his person such kindness that there was no mistaking him for a foe or an exploiter.

Those he cured helped to spread the news about this miracle man. Still, tensions sometimes arose and the Doctor's patience was put to trial.

"What a blockhead I was to come to these savages!" he exclaimed one day in sudden desperation over a native who had left the hospital carrying away with him his sick child. Whereupon Joseph looked up from his work and quietly remarked: "Yes, Doctor, here on earth you are a blockhead, but not in heaven . . ."

The hardest thing for the natives to understand was that they would not get something for nothing. In exchange for his services, Schweitzer exacted, or tried to exact, a contribution in kind—not for himself, of course, but for his hospital. Labor was high on the list—indeed it was essential if the hospital were to be kept going. But here he met with a great deal of opposition. The natives had a peculiar attitude toward work. To the white man's mind they were simply lazy. Perhaps they were. But their underlying reason for being so was entirely different from ours. They would work long enough to satisfy a need of the moment. They would, for example, paddle for hours in the murderous heat when they had to. But when Schweitzer told them that in Europe and America people canoed for pleasure, they laughed. They could not believe it.

A true child of nature, the native was a free man. Like a child he needed authority and love. Schweitzer's formula was: "I am your brother, but I am your elder brother."

Even though he understood their reasons, they could drive Schweitzer to utter despair. One day he started a group of natives on an urgent job and went back to his patients. Returning sometime later, he found the job untouched. He exploded. "Why do you shout at us, Doctor?" asked the natives. "Stay with us and we will work, but when you are in the hospital or somewhere else, why should we work?" Again and again he had to use patience, persuasion, friendliness, and energy.

This is how the Doctor musician describes the felling of trees:

"The day passes like a symphony.

"LENTO: Grim-looking natives are given knives and axes at the landing station. They advance at snail pace toward the trees.

"MODERATO: Axes and knives move slowly; the conductor vainly tries to quicken the movements. Then it is time for the midday meal.

"ADAGIO: Reluctantly the workers are brought back to the area in the damp forest. Not a breath of air. From time to time one hears a stroke ring out.

"SCHERZO: I am successful with a few jokes which I try out in my despair. The atmosphere becomes lighter. Gay words are exchanged. Some of the natives start singing. It also grows a little cooler.

"FINALE: Merriment has overcome all of them. Now they are going to show it to this evil forest, which is the cause of their being here instead of lolling in the hospital. The forest shall pay for it! Wild oaths are heard. With shrieks and boos they attack it; axes and knives move frantically. Now no bird must fly, no squirrel pass; no question must be asked, no order must be given. The slightest interruption would break the spell. Luckily nothing interferes; the wild activity continues. When the 'finale' can be made to last half an hour, the day has not been lost. It only stops when I cry: 'Amani, amani!' (Enough, enough!) and put an end to the work."

Natives differed from white men in many other ways. Their attitude toward property in the words of Joseph was simply: "All that lies in the open belongs to all. Only what is locked is respected." Many things disappeared which were completely useless to the natives. A most valuable portion of Bach's "St. Matthew's Passion," which Schweitzer had carefully annotated for the organ, disappeared for no other reason than that it lay on the piano. . . . So, to his great annoyance, the good Doctor was obliged to lock everything away and he carried with him wherever he went a fat bunch of keys.

With all their overwhelming fears, there was one fear that the natives did not know—the fear of death. Death was the law of nature and they accepted it naturally. Schweitzer had many occasions to be impressed by this attitude.

But then, the natives were also unafraid of fire; they completely ignored its dangers. They had an excellent reason for this: the humidity of the jungle prevented fires from spreading. The natives always had a fire burning in their huts. They cooked their meals on it. It protected them against mosquitoes and kept away the wild beasts. It also kept their huts warm at night. But when the Doctor first saw fire burning right under the cot of a patient, he was terrified. Through his interpreter he prohibited all fires. But the fires continued to burn and with time Schweitzer became accustomed to the once frightening idea. On the other hand, the natives never tired of listening to Schweitzer's tale about the big fires that devastated whole forests in Europe and America. It made them laugh as if it were a fairy tale.

Against fear and superstition Schweitzer could do nothing or extremely little. And so he concentrated on fighting the diseases of the body. But with the growing numbers of the sick, he needed more help and more space. He could not continue operating in a chicken coop; it was vitally important to have a real hospital.

The heads of the Missions were to hold a conference in a distant village called Samkita. Albert Schweitzer decided to make the journey. It was his first long canoe trip and he thoroughly enjoyed the experience. It was still dark and cool when he and two missionaries left Lambaréné. They took pineapples to quench their thirst and big bunches of bananas to eat on the way.

Schweitzer also took a case full of tobacco leaves instead of bank notes to pay his crew, and he sat on top of the box in order to prevent its precious contents from being stolen. Tobacco made from these leaves was very strong and the natives smoked with passion in the daytime and also at night, when they could not sleep. Promise the crew so many leaves of tobacco and you were sure to reach your destination a couple of hours faster!

Sunrise brought out the heat and the dreaded

tsetse flies, greedy for human blood. For some reason the only protection against them was white clothes. The two men who wore white suits were scarcely molested. The suit of the third one was yellow and he was badly bitten. The worst sufferers, of course, were the natives who wore no clothes.

The journey was slow in the exhausting heat. On their way they had to paddle around hippopotamuses floating threateningly right under the surface of the water. Except during these tense and silent moments, the paddlers sang to while away the time. Most of the songs were improvised. They chanted about the landscape. Passing near a village, they sang about their passengers and their destination. Off and on they sang until nightfall came and they had finally reached Samkita.

Schweitzer greatly enjoyed the company of the assembled missionaries. ". . . How inspiring it was to work with men who for years had renounced so much in order to devote themselves to the services of those who had so little. . . ." In his great modesty, Schweitzer did not include himself—though he had renounced as much and more.

The journey was a success: Schweitzer returned with a modest but helpful sum of money for a hospital building. He had also been able to exchange the land he had received from the Paris mission for a more convenient location closer to the landing place.

Upon his return he was fortunate to find some workers and immediately began to clear the ground. But with their first pay the workers disappeared to drink and did not reappear. Albert Schweitzer and Joseph were left alone to carry on the task.

They had barely finished clearing a space in the jungle when Schweitzer received an urgent message to come to a desperately sick mission woman from another village. It was days before he was able to return. Nearing Lambaréné he thought he saw a mirage: a corrugated iron building stood in the clearing! The miracle had been performed by two mission workers, Joseph, and a few well natives staying at the hospital with their sick relatives.

It was a great joy—not only because of the work done, but because now he had proof that his teachings and his example had done something to convince the people of the necessity to help themselves.

Soon afterwards the first hospital of Lambaréné opened its doors. It was nothing like the hospitals in our country. A big barrack built of wooden poles and corrugated iron, it had a large dormitory for the sick and their families, and a surgery room. The floors were made of cement, the shelves of precious rosewood and mahogany. A small building outside served as a waiting room.

The beds were made of lumber and jungle vines, the mattresses of dry grass. Actually, a shortage of beds was one problem Schweitzer did not have. The natives were accustomed to sleeping on the ground. Often enough on his rounds he found the healthy relative in bed, while the sick man lay on the floor, where he felt more at ease!

The new hospital attracted more sick and brought another problem: food shortage. Every native was expected to bring some food, but most of them never did. Schweitzer resorted to threats: "I will not accept those who do not bring their share of food!" he thundered in a stern voice. But the natives had come to know the Doctor's kindness and, sure he would never send away a sick person, they turned up with empty hands and empty stomachs. Not only that, but many of them expected the doctor to present them with food when they left the hospital! Were they not by then his friends? Well, the custom of the jungle was to give your departing friends a farewell gift.

Still, some of the patients were eager to show their gratitude. A man who had had an operation saved twenty francs, as he put it, "to pay the doctor for the expensive thread with which he sewed up my stomach."

Food in the region of Lambaréné was scarce. The natives' diet consisted mainly of bananas and manioc. Manioc, the root of the cassava plant, was the local equivalent of bread. Cut into long strips, it was cooked over the fire. Bananas in this region were large and nutritious, but not tasteful when raw; they had to be cooked. The natives loved meat but ate it rarely, for hunting in the jungle was both difficult and dangerous. It was not that they were hard to please. Every kind of meat was considered a feast—monkey, snake, or elephant. The only meat they were reluctant to eat was lion. As one native explained to Schweitzer, "The lion I eat may have eaten my grandfather."

Europeans, incidentally, were equally reluctant to eat monkey, the easiest to obtain of the local game. It almost seemed a first step to cannibalism!

It was customary for the natives to go on fishing expeditions once every year and for a number of days they gorged themselves on fish —cooked or raw. Many traditional rituals were performed to appease the evil spirits so they would not spoil the catch.

Schweitzer wanted to give the natives a more varied diet and he decided to plant vegetables on the grounds of the hospital. As usual, he had to set the example—and doing this he became an enthusiastic gardener.

Although Schweitzer had promised to remain "mute as a fish" on all theological questions, he was invited by the missionaries and the native preachers to preach at their assemblies. It was a great joy.

He preached in the open before an attentive circle of natives—and pelicans and other animals that crept out of the jungle to join the congregation. Every sentence was translated by a native teacher into the two main languages, Galoan and Pahuin. After the sermon, Schweitzer frequently discussed Christian principles with his parishioners.

Once he asked a native woman whether she thought the Lord Jesus was rich or poor. "What a stupid question," she answered. "If God, the Great Chief, was His father, he certainly could not have been poor!"

Already a preacher, carpenter, gardener, and a philosopher in his spare time, the good Doctor often had to function as a judge. He intervened in the endless palavers and decided who was right or wrong.

Natives who arrived by canoe were expected to supply the hospital with fresh fish. One night a native took a canoe without asking the owner's permission and went fishing. Upon his return the angry owner was on the landing to claim his canoe and the catch! It was his by right, he shouted. The two began to fight. Schweitzer was called. He listened to both sides and then pronounced the verdict:

"You are both in the right and also in the wrong. You, as owner of the canoe," he said to the first one, "are in the right, because he should have asked permission to use it. Therefore you are entitled to a third of his catch. But you are also in the wrong on two counts: You should have fastened your canoe with a padlock, as you have been shown. And you are guilty of laziness—there was good moonlight for fishing and you stayed in bed!"

Then he turned to the other: "You were wrong in taking the canoe without permission, so you owe the owner a third of the fish. But you were right in making use of the moonlight to go fishing. Therefore you are entitled to a third of what you caught. And the hospital is entitled to a third, because it took place on our grounds and you have taken some of the Doctor's time in adjusting this dispute!"

Schweitzer found that many native customs which at first shocked the Western visitor as barbarous seemed much less so when one came to know the reasons for them. Polygamy, for example, was explained this way: Because there was no cow or other milk, the native mother was obliged to nurse her child till it was three or more years old. Motherhood was considered sacred among the natives. So long as she was needed, a mother was expected to devote herself entirely to her child. Inasmuch as during these long years the man needed someone to look after his hut, to tend to his fields, to cook his food, he took a second wife.

Now, a wife in the Gabon was not to be had for the asking. She cost a great deal of money. A man had to buy his wife from the girl's father, paying whatever sum was demanded of him. Visitors who objected to such a procedure were quietly reminded by Schweitzer that it was not unlike the dowry of other countries. "The only difference," he added, "is that here it is the bridegroom who pays the bill, while in your country he is the one to get the money!"

Joseph, with whom Schweitzer talked about everything, bitterly complained that he did not have the money to buy himself a new wife, now that his first wife had deserted him. "Of course," he explained, "I could pay her off in installments, but this is no good. A wife will never respect her husband as long as she has not been fully paid for."

As he came to know the natives, Schweitzer learned about their kindness, their friendliness, and their strong family feeling. He found also that they had an innate sense of right and wrong.

Of course, their conception of right and wrong was different from that of the white man. But was not their world, the nature in which they lived, a completely different one?

Without ever imposing his moral views upon them, Albert Schweitzer gradually, patiently,

made them understand the principles of brotherhood and the necessity of working. If he succeeded where others had failed, it was because
he taught by example. Dressed in ordinary
working clothes, he chopped trees, dug irrigation ditches, built barracks, planted vegetables
alongside the natives. This was not the way
other Europeans behaved.

There was something else that helped pro-
mote mutual understanding: Albert Schweitzer's never-failing sense of humor. To the
delight of the natives, he was always ready for a
good laugh. In his diary Schweitzer describes
many situations that aroused his merriment.
One day, for example, as he was chopping a tree,
the young relative of a hospital patient passed
by.

Schweitzer called, "Say, friend, will you not
lend us a hand?"

The native, who had just returned from
school, replied, "I am an intellectual; I am not
a worker."

"You are lucky," Schweitzer retorted. "I, too,

wanted to be an intellectual, but I did not succeed!"

Once, in relaxed mood, he wrote to friends: "If my life were to be finished by the cannibals, I hope they would write on my tombstone: 'We have eaten Dr. Schweitzer—He was good to the end!'"

After a day of exhausting physical work it was good to relax. Here in the jungle there were no places to go to, no social gatherings, no telephone calls, hardly a newspaper. When papers came, it seemed queer to read the outdated headlines. It was weeks, often months, before papers reached Lambaréné. The jungle was immense and of necessity communications were rare and uncertain. Entertainment had to be found within oneself. Schweitzer read philosophical and scientific books, wrote, and meditated.

In the past his greatest joy had always been music. When he made his great decision to go to Africa, giving up this pleasure had been the greatest sacrifice of all. He thought that total renunciation, painful as it was, would be easier if he allowed his fingers to become rusty.

But the Paris Bach Society, whose beloved and admired member he had been for so many years, took another view of the matter. They thought that now, more than ever before, Schweitzer would need music. A special organ-piano, zinc-lined to withstand the tropical climate, was made and sent to Lambaréné. It stood, silently, in the little house, waiting for the Doctor to change his mind.

For a long time Schweitzer gave himself entirely to his missionary and medical work, convinced that the resources of his body were inexhaustible. But this was not Gunsbach, or Paris, or Strasbourg—and he was not twenty years old any more. In Lambaréné a stifling steam covered everything; sweat poured from the body. Despite the climate, day after day Schweitzer worked from before sunrise to long after sunset—and this was not ordinary work. To endure the sight of suffering, dying men every day was sometimes more than even he could stand.

One evening he felt he could bear it no longer; he had to find some way of escape, some source of inspiration. He went to his piano, sat down, lifted the lid and started to play Bach. He had found the way back to his enchanted world.

From then on, during the short midday rest period, on Sunday afternoons, and often late into the night, Schweitzer played the piano. Over the years he learned by heart the great compositions of Bach, Mendelssohn, César Franck, and many others. To immerse himself in their spiritual world revived him both in body and in mind. It was a great blessing.

6

Enemy Alien

In the remoteness of the African jungle, news of war came sparingly. Rumors of impending hostilities were spread by the traders of the nearby villages, who heard them from the travelers arriving by freight boats. Mail from Europe brought increasingly bad news.

And then, in August, 1914, war broke out between Germany and France.

Born in Alsace, which still belonged to Germany, Albert Schweitzer was a German citizen. In Lambaréné, a French colony, he became an enemy alien.

One day a patrol of native guards arrived at the hospital. Armed with guns, they carried an order from the French Governor restricting the movements of the Schweitzers. They must immediately abandon all medical work, stop all communication with the natives. He and his wife were prisoners of war.

It was a calamitous situation. How could he explain it to the natives? From one day to another, a man who had devoted himself solely to the service of all, who had harmed none, suddenly was placed under arrest like a criminal. How strangely did white men act! Had not Schweitzer told them again and again that white people were their brothers? What had they done with the spirit of Christian love which made them send money and medicines to Lambaréné? White Christians were killing each other and the Doctor was a prisoner. They were bewildered.

The damage done to the Christian cause was immense. To Schweitzer nationality, race, or creed mattered little—to him there were only human beings. He loved the meadows and the forests of his childhood, the bells of his village church. Yet he loved them not as an Alsatian, or a Frenchman, or a German, but as a human being. He was heartbroken at the thought of all the misery the war would bring to the people he knew and to all those he did not know.

The heart of this great humanitarian bled for all, regardless of the color of their skin, their nationality, or their religion. To call Albert Schweitzer an enemy alien, was truly a paradox. He was a member of the family of man and no one's enemy. But he stood alone, or very nearly so, in a world bitterly divided by war. Born on the "wrong" side of a borderline, he was now the victim of the circumstances of his birth—a prisoner within the walls of his little house.

A lesser man might have broken under the strain. But Albert Schweitzer, drawing upon the seemingly infinite resources of his being, now put his mind to work. Forbidden to practice medicine, he began to write. On the very day when the sentry took up its post in front of his house, Schweitzer sat down at his desk.

"We are living today under the sign of the collapse of civilization," he wrote as the first sentence of his *Philosophy of Civilization*.

A man could not set himself a harder task. From morning to night Albert Schweitzer thought and wrote, thought and wrote—while the hospital stood empty and silent. But this unnatural situation could not last.

One day a native arrived, bearing a word from the Governor. Schweitzer carefully examined the note. Why did the Governor bother sending a messenger with so insignificant a message? A look at the messenger's face produced an explanation: the man was obviously sick. The government in Paris had sent orders forbidding Schweitzer to practice because he was an alien. The Governor could not disobey orders, but, with no other doctor around, he always found a way to send Schweitzer "important" messages by sick messengers, who were, of course, then treated by the good Doctor. And soon one ailing messenger followed the other—the bitter need for medical help was stronger than war regulations!

In the meantime, in Paris, Schweitzer's devoted friends had been hard at work. They wrote petitions and intervened on behalf of the Doctor and his cause. Within three months Schweitzer was set free and allowed to resume his hospital work.

Needless to say, medical supplies dwindled fast and so did Schweitzer's gold reserve. He borrowed money from the Missionary Society. But as the war years went by, it became increasingly difficult to find the much-needed surgical and medical supplies.

Joseph, whom Schweitzer was no longer able to pay, left. German submarines were blockading the sea lanes and food supplies no longer arrived from Europe. So many natives had been conscripted that there was a shortage of labor; little food was raised locally.

The Schweitzers lived on a meager diet of rice and fruit. Every effort was made to feed the patients. Cut off from the world, the Schweitzers found the tiniest, most insignificant items

above: The little church in the Alsatian village of Gunsbach where Dr. Schweitzer's father was minister for forty years.

left: The organ in the Gunsbach church, built according to Dr. Schweitzer's specifications, and which he prizes above all other organs.

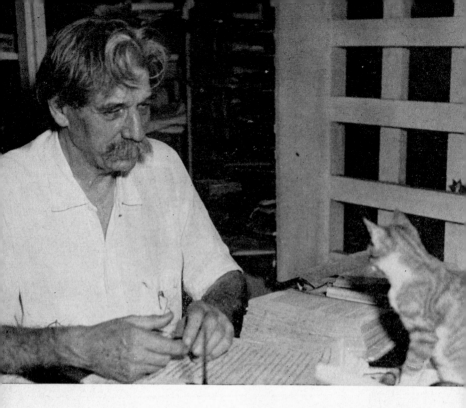

Dr. Schweitzer at his desk in Lambaréné, with his pet cat, Sisi.

opposite page:

top: View of the hospital from the river.

bottom: Arrival of patients at the hospital.

The main street of the hospital. The operating and consulting rooms are on the left; the post-operative wards on the right. Patients await their turn for treatment.

Dr. Schweitzer holds the screen while an assistant hammers it in place. The screen must be put on very carefully if it is to keep out the insects.

above: The landing place of native pirogues at the jungle hospital of Dr. Albert Schweitzer.

left: Dr. Schweitzer with Jean-Baptiste, one of his pet antelopes.

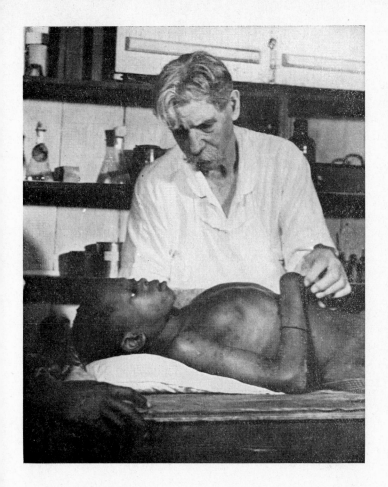

Anxiety and compassion are expressed in Dr. Schweitzer's face as he bends over to examine a new young patient.

opposite page:

top: A chameleon brought to him by the natives is making friends with the doctor.

bottom: A litter case being carried through the main street to the hospital.

Arrival of the river boat bringing cases of medicine, rice, and wood to the hospital. Most of these supplies are donations of friends of the hospital.

In the hot jungle night, Dr. Schweitzer, at his piano, prepares for the recordings he will make in Europe at the console of the Gunsbach organ.

Dr. Schweitzer being interviewed by Anita Daniel on the occasion of his first trip to the United States. *Photo by Pix.*

became precious in this wilderness. There were no limits to thrift. When Christmas came, Schweitzer lighted a few small candles on the palm tree—the African Christmas tree. But he allowed them to burn only half way. Carefully saved, they were stored away for the following Christmas, when they helped bring still another glimmer of holiday hope to war-shadowed Lambaréné.

The longer it lasted, the more difficult it became to explain the war to the natives. These were questions that concerned them directly. For now young men were shipped to Europe to serve with the colonial army—many of them never to return. One day Schweitzer was visiting a village when conscripts were embarking for the war. When the river boat had left:

". . . The crowd dispersed," recalled Albert Schweitzer, "but on the riverbank an old woman, whose son had been taken, sat weeping silently. I took her hand and tried to comfort her, but she went on crying as if she did not hear me . . ." Tears also ran from Albert

Schweitzer's eyes. It was the first time he had openly cried since he had been stung by a bee at the age of two. He stood by the grieving woman and wept; there was nothing else he could do.

Why do Europeans wage war against each other? the natives wanted to know. Could not the chiefs of their tribes meet and talk things over? And how could they afford to pay for all their dead? The savages would shake their heads over the cruelty of the Europeans who seemed to kill each other for no reason at all— they did not even eat their dead.

Slow as it was, from time to time mail reached Lambaréné. Now it brought sad news: Albert Schweitzer's mother was dead. She had been killed—trampled to death by the horses of the German cavalry as she walked along the street of her Alsatian village.

Pain gripped Albert Schweitzer's heart. In Europe there was death and destruction; all around him, fear, sickness and death. What good was all his work? He labored trying to save one life while thousands were being killed daily. Was it worth it?

Yes—for so long as a man breathes there is hope, and no physician worthy of his name would abandon him. Now humanity was sick. The philosopher was also a doctor—he must diagnose the sickness of mankind.

7

The Great Revelation

His heart full of grief, his head full of daily
worries, Albert Schweitzer went about his tasks
as usual from daybreak to sundown. But after
his work was done, when only the cries of the
wild animals interrupted the deep silence of
the jungle night, he wrestled with the ever-
recurring question which preyed so heavily on
his mind: Was there a key to the understanding
of life?

The books on religion and philosophy he had read were filled with beautiful and noble principles. "Thou shalt not kill . . ." and yet, men killed. Why did those great ideas fail to inspire mankind?

Progress and its new inventions produced bigger and better arms leading to ever greater destruction, instead of preventing war. Why?

He struggled, often despairingly, to answer these colossal questions.

"I seemed to myself to be like a man who has to build a new and better boat to replace a rotten one in which he can no longer trust himself to the sea, and yet does not know how to begin."

How could inhumanity develop along with progress? Often, he mused, animals were more human than humans themselves. They never killed each other unless they were in need of food, or when forced to defend their young ones.

At times it seemed to him that he was reaching the light, and yet . . . "I was leaning with all my might against an iron door which would not yield."

And then, in April, 1915, Schweitzer left on a long journey to see the ailing wife of a missionary. Aboard the small boat crowded with natives he was the only white man. Very slowly the boat made its way between the sand banks. Schweitzer sat on the deck, lost in his thoughts, struggling to find the answer. He held a pencil in his hand. He had covered whole sheets of paper with doodles and unconnected sentences, when suddenly. . . .

"Late on the third day, at the very moment when, at sunset, we were making our way through a herd of hippopotamuses, there flashed upon my mind, unforeseen and unsought, the phrase: *Reverence for life* . . . The iron door had yielded, the path in the thicket had become visible. Now I had found my way."

"Reverence for life," three simple words containing the vision of a better world. What was reverence for life? The Bible says: "I am life which wills to live in the midst of life, which wills to live."

This is not only true of the relations between

MONON PUBLIC LIBRARY

men—it is also true of animals and plants.

But man cannot live without destroying life. So what is he to do?

To live, a man must eat. But, says Schweitzer, he must strive never to destroy the life of animal or plant except when he is hungry. And he must never kill a man or an animal unless he is attacked and forced to do so to protect his own life or that of his children, friends, or family.

"Whenever I injure life of any kind, I must be quite clear whether it is necessary or not. I ought never to pass the limits of the unavoidable, even in apparently insignificant cases. The countryman who has mowed down a thousand blossoms in his meadow as fodder for his cows should take care on the way home he does not, in wanton pastime, switch off the head of a single flower growing on the edge of the road. For in doing so, he injures life without being forced to do so by necessity."

This is what reverence for life means.

When Schweitzer saw an earthworm on his path, he carefully avoided stepping on it. But if he encountered a poisonous snake on the hospital grounds, he killed it, for it was a threat to everybody.

To carry out this resolution to respect life demands a constant effort. Schweitzer says: ". . . all of us ought to feel what a horrible thing it is to cause suffering and death out of mere thoughtlessness. At the bottom of our heart we all think this, but we fail to acknowledge it and to carry our belief into practice, chiefly because we are afraid of being laughed at by other people as sentimentalists. . . ." And he urges: "Start thinking when you are young and you will never stop thinking."

It takes more courage to respect life than to destroy it. Faith and love, the weapons Schweitzer chose, were much more difficult to use than guns.

"Reverence for life" was the key that Albert Schweitzer had found to open minds and hearts to cure humanity. He knew now how he would write his book about civilization. When he returned to his hospital, he was like a man who had won a great battle.

Meanwhile in Europe the war was going on. A new order from the French government arrived: all enemy aliens were to be transferred to France for the duration of the war. A messenger from the Governor arrived: The Schweitzers must leave Lambaréné.

There was little time. The steamer with many prisoners aboard was waiting at the landing. But Schweitzer could not leave before he talked to the sick and told them himself that he must go.

He packed a few belongings. He entrusted his manuscript on civilization to the care of a missionary. Amid general consternation, a canoe pulled up alongside the steamer. A man was brought to the hospital; he was moaning with pain. Schweitzer obtained permission to perform his last operation. Then, with Mrs. Schweitzer, wearily he boarded the little white steamer that four and one-half years earlier had brought him to Lambaréné.

8

Prisoner of War

Aboard the French steamer *Afrique*, the Schweitzers were confined to a small cabin and strictly forbidden to talk to anyone except the steward assigned to them. Both were so worn out by the hardships of these long African years that neither was eager for conversation.

To occupy his mind and to make full use of his time, as usual, Albert Schweitzer began to work. In the small cabin there was no place for even a table. Write, he could not; so he decided to learn by heart some of Bach's fugues and Widor's *Sixth Organ Symphony*. He used the top of his trunk as an imaginary organ and pressed imaginary pedals on the cabin floor. It was an effort, but he could not be idle. Besides, working on his music prevented Schweitzer from brooding over the dark future that lay ahead.

In Bordeaux the prisoners of war were kept in temporary barracks before being assigned to camps. Here Schweitzer came down with dysentery. He was not entirely well when he and his wife were taken to a large internment camp in the Pyrenees Mountains at Garaison. Garaison in the local dialect means healing, but the long-disused and cold monastery certainly belied its name.

When the prison guard searched the prisoners, he found a book in Albert Schweitzer's pocket: "Politics" by Aristotle. He was furious. "How dare you bring a political book here? Don't you know it's strictly forbidden?" When

Schweitzer politely informed him that this book had been written by a Greek philosopher thousands of years before, the guard would not believe it until it was confirmed to him by other officials. Then he mumbled, "Well, I didn't know they knew about politics so long ago. All right, you can keep that book."

There were too many internees packed into the cold, humid, bare cells. Even so, Schweitzer found stimulation in the daily contact with people of all classes and nationalities. There were Arabs, Greeks, Chinese, Africans, Argentines, Indians, Germans, and Turks with their veiled wives. They came from every walk of life: scholars, shoemakers, artists, bankers, cooks, engineers, tailors, priests and carpenters. There was also a gypsy orchestra that had been playing in a Paris night club. Its leader had heard of the famous musician, Albert Schweitzer. He was so happy to meet him in person that he invited Schweitzer to join the gypsy orchestra as an honorary member. A few weeks later one of the gypsies learned that it was Mrs. Schweitzer's birthday and they all serenaded at the window of her cell with their wild, enchanting melodies.

Another prisoner, Berkeloh by name, had been in Lambaréné, where Schweitzer had saved the life of his sick wife. Was there anything he could do to repay his debt? To show his gratitude, Berkeloh built a table for Schweitzer that enabled him to resume writing.

Among all the trades and professions represented at Garaison, there was only one physician: Albert Schweitzer. The camp's medical service consisted of an elderly man hardly able to cope with his work. In no time at all Albert Schweitzer was busy practicing medicine and even dentistry.

In his free time he talked: "One needed no books to learn much. I made full use of my opportunities to learn from men with specialized knowledge of banking, architecture, factory-building and equipment, cereal-growing, furnace-making, and many other things that came to be of use to me later."

He worked and studied all through that long winter, giving generously of his time to his fellow prisoners. But his health was badly damaged. A transfer to another camp in the south of France did little to improve his condition.

The sudden, glad news of his release was truly a godsend. An exchange of prisoners was to take place. The Schweitzers were on the list. They were free to return to Alsace. Since the war was not ended, they had to make a long detour to enter Alsace through neutral Switzerland. The train ran no farther than Colmar. From here the Schweitzers—both in miserable physical condition and carrying heavy bundles —walked up the valley home to Gunsbach.

It was no longer the peaceful village of Schweitzer's childhood. The battlefield was near; gunfire could be heard day and night. The aged minister was there to meet them; father and son embraced in silence. But even the warm atmosphere of his home did not help to speed Schweitzer's recovery. Not only was he exhausted from his long years of work and the debilitating climate of Africa, he was also a very sick man.

Schweitzer had to undergo an operation, and

this was done in the hospital of nearby Colmar. For once, he who only knew how to take care of others was forced to let others take care of him.

At last, after four years of bitter war, the Armistice was signed on November 11, 1918. Schweitzer was only half recovered when he agreed to work in the ward of a Strasbourg hospital. The pay was very small, but he felt happy to get it. It allowed him to provide for his wife, who was expecting a child. In his rare free moments, he continued to write his "Philosophy of Civilization" and to work on various religious subjects.

But he could not forget Lambaréné. In his thoughts, he returned time and again to his jungle hospital. What had happened to all his poor sick Negroes? Had all his work been in vain?

He was also worried about the debts he had made in Lambaréné, when he had borrowed money to buy medical supplies for the sick. He decided to use all his energy to secure the necessary money to repay his friends and to go back to Africa to resume the task he had started.

From now on he accepted every single invitation to play the organ in the churches of France, Spain, England and Germany. He had not been able to practice since he had become a prisoner and he was afraid of disappointing his public. But the welcome he received everywhere was such that he found the courage to go on with his recitals.

Before long he received an invitation from an unexpected source: the Archbishop Soederblom of Sweden remembered that promising young theologian and philosopher Albert Schweitzer. He had followed his career with great interest and now he invited Schweitzer and his wife to come to Sweden. He wrote to them that it was an ideal place to recover from all their hardships, and food was plentiful. (Sweden had remained neutral in the First World War.) He could lecture about Africa at the Swedish University of Upsala and play the organ in Swedish churches.

With alacrity Schweitzer accepted. His simple straightforward account of his life in the jungle and the joy it gave him to alleviate human suffering greatly impressed his audiences. Whether he spoke or played the organ, his reception everywhere was enthusiastic.

Archbishop Soederblom encouraged Schweitzer to write a book about his African experience. Schweitzer wrote *On the Edge of the Primeval Forest,* which was translated into many languages, bringing him considerable renown and also considerable sums of money. He could now repay his friends, and he had money enough to go back to Africa.

The war was over. From Lambaréné came more and more letters urging Schweitzer to return, telling him how desperately he was needed. He listened to those voices and he listened to his inner voice, which clearly said, "Go. . . ."

There were other artists who could play the organ, others who could teach and write in Europe. But there was not a single doctor within hundreds of miles of Lambaréné.

His decision was not easy to take. His daughter Rhena was still a little baby; his wife was not fully recovered. They must stay in Europe where they could have good care. He would return alone to Lambaréné.

He gave a few more concerts to raise money for medical supplies. He took a few courses in dentistry. Then, on February 21, 1924, accompanied by a young medical student from England, Noel Gillespie, Albert Schweitzer sailed back to Africa.

9
Lambaréné Revisited

His excitement was great. What had become of the hospital? He had not expected to find it in exactly the state he had left it, but what he saw when the canoe finally docked at the landing brought tears to his eyes.

The jungle grew thick over all that he had cleared by the sweat of his brow. Rust had eaten through the corrugated iron. Nothing was left of the roof. It was a catastrophe!

Recovering from the shock, Schweitzer with Noel Gillespie, took a canoe and journeyed from one village to another in search of the precious roof "tiles." He knew from experience how hard they were to get. Made of raffia woven over bamboo sticks, their making required great skill. But skilled natives preferred to work for the lumber camps where the pay was better.

Without a protecting roof, there could be no hospital. Schweitzer used diplomacy and even threats. The patients, who had started to swarm in from all sides at the news of their Doctor's return, were told they must "pay" in "tiles."

Little by little, after months of patient waiting—and not a few painful sunstrokes—Schweitzer had his hospital back in shape. All the old problems had to be faced again: food and labor must be found. To his great relief, thanks to his growing fame in Europe, a most efficient Alsatian nurse, Mathilde Kottmann, arrived to help the doctor. She was a priceless acquisition! Soon she was followed by Dr. Nessman, a surgeon. Schweitzer was no longer alone to cope with his tremendous responsibilities.

But each day brought its own worry and usually more than one: continuous struggle against ignorance and superstition, fighting against the wild beasts and the murderous insects. And the sick poured in. New tribes arrived; the number of languages increased, and there was no interpreter! For Joseph was now working in a factory, and no other interpreter had been found.

One day a young boy of the Benjabi tribe was rushed in for an emergency operation. On the operating table, his face suddenly became rigid with horror. He had fallen into the hands of the dreaded cannibals! They were going to kill him and eat him. Those knives could mean nothing else. And there was no one who could tell him in his own language that it was not so. Only the beautiful smile on the Doctor's face helped to alleviate his fear. Schweitzer said that he never had felt such deep emotion before using the operating knife. The boy was saved and his happiness and relief were Schweitzer's greatest reward.

The hospital grew and grew, and so did the load of responsibilities. There came famine, epidemics of dysentery. There was nothing Schweitzer could do to convince the natives of the danger of contamination. Against his strictest orders, the well mingled with the sick, shared their food with them, and spread the disease. Finally he was forced to build an iron fence to isolate the sick.

The Doctor and his staff worked harder than ever, but it was not humanly possible to give all the sick the care they needed. So Schweitzer wrote letters to Europe pleading for more helpers. To his great joy, two fine doctors and another wonderful nurse, Emma Hausknecht, arrived. Now at last with this little group, he could start community work. He could also confess to himself how completely exhausted he was.

He started plans to enlarge the hospital and build stockrooms for medical supplies. All the improvements were designed to fit the needs of the natives. He wanted them to feel at home in the hospital, to be happy. For this reason, he would not have electricity and other modern improvements which would have made work easier for himself and for his staff, but which would have created a foreign atmosphere for the natives.

10

Schweitzer's Animal World

Lambaréné was not only the famous hospital in the jungle. It was also the haven of animals. From near and far, sick, old, tame, and wild animals found their way to Schweitzer. They were brought by natives; Schweitzer picked them up on his walks. Some simply appeared out of the jungle. Sick animals were nursed to health until they were well enough to return to the forest.

Having tasted the life of Lambaréné, some of them chose to stay; others left only to come back. Parakeets, goats, porcupines, cats, antelopes, chickens, chimpanzees, pelicans—all lived here together in perfect harmony.

Like Saint Francis, Albert Schweitzer had a way with animals. Wherever he went, they surrounded him as if they knew that with him they were perfectly safe. And how right they were! Everyone in Lambaréné had learned that the life of every single animal was sacred, including that of the harmless insects.

Many of the jungle insects, it must be repeated, were more terrible than the wild beasts. For example, Schweitzer had built the chicken coop close to his house. Thus, at night when he heard the frightful shrieks of his chickens, rendered mad with fear at the first warnings of advancing masses of ants, he could rush to their help. If he did not stop the onslaught, the ants would march on. Like a powerful army under the leadership of a great general, they divided into five or six columns, surrounding the chicken coop on all sides. They swarmed in through the tiniest crevices by the thousands. They attacked the chickens at the throat with their fierce mandibles, choking them to death.

At the first alarm, Schweitzer and his helpers jumped out of their beds. They grabbed the sprayers, standing ready for such emergencies, and ran out to fight off the attack. They sprayed the ants with gasoline or kerosene to disperse them. It was by no means a pleasant task. Lightly clad, the spraying squad suffered painful bites from the furious ants. Schweitzer once counted as many as fifty of them clinging to his body. Having fought off a first attack, often Schweitzer fell asleep only to be awakened again by the bleating of the terrified goats, which were the victims of a renewed attack by the formidable ants.

Monkeys were more fun. Young Upsi, the Doctor's pet chimpanzee, was often found stealing eggs from the chicken coop. When a freshly laid egg was taken from a hen, it was customary to quiet her by substituting a china egg. One day the Doctor saw Upsi furiously trying to bite into the china egg. It looked so funny that Schweitzer laughed out loud. "For many days Upsi avoided me, which I understood perfectly well, because I had seen him being made a fool of," wrote Schweitzer in his diary.

With all his burdens, Schweitzer never forgot his animals. On the hospital staff there was a young blind man, whose name was Mongo. Schweitzer had found him dying of sleeping sickness and had saved his life. He had to be allotted some work, so Mongo's task was to feed a lame fish hawk. Every morning the sightless man sat by the river with his fishing rod until he had caught the daily ration of fish for the waiting bird.

Elephants, Schweitzer learned, were peaceful and harmless animals as long as they were not disturbed, wounded or excited in some way. If they were molested, they were capable of destroying everything in sight. They would throw a man into the air and gore him with their tusks or trample him to death. The elephants' favorite sport (and a great nuisance for the white settlers!) was to walk along the telegraph lines and pull out all the poles, one by one.

The huge hippopotamuses were much feared by the natives. They were a constant threat to the canoes and had to be most carefully avoided. Once Schweitzer was in a hurry and asked his paddlers to go faster. Reluctantly they obeyed. Suddenly hippopotamuses appeared so close to the canoe that only by a miracle did the little group save their lives. Schweitzer had had his lesson. The jungle was no place for rushing. Every jungle experience with nature as well as with people taught him the need for patience—endless patience.

Schweitzer had his special private circle of animals; they were his pets. He loved them dearly. In his little room at night, when he was busy thinking and writing, his big cat sat on the desk. At his feet lay the dog, Caramba, while in the next room was the lame antelope. A pig with its piglets slept in front of the door.

Schweitzer had infinite love and understanding for his pets. Once he found that the cat had torn up the manuscript which he had been working on for weeks. He laughed. "What should a cat know about a manuscript, except that it was paper to play with?"

11

Activities in Europe

Schweitzer's new hospital was finally ready. January 21, 1927, was the great day when the sick were moved into the new building. The moving was greatly facilitated by a motorboat recently arrived from Sweden. It was a most welcome gift from a group of Swedish ladies, ardent admirers of Schweitzer, whom he had met while he was lecturing in their country.

This motorboat certainly meant a great deal to the community of Lambaréné. Until then small canoes were the only means of transportation. Schweitzer christened the boat *Taksamyket*, which in Swedish means "Thank you."

That evening Schweitzer made his first round of the new hospital. Families were gaily cooking meals while their sick rested in comfortable, clean beds. Everywhere Schweitzer saw smiling faces. "Doctor, this is a good hut, a good hut!" He was deeply moved. A great step forward had been made.

Gratitude for friends all over the world filled his heart. Their gifts had made possible the building of the hospital; and without the fine devoted services of his doctors and nurses he could never have accomplished all this.

Now Schweitzer could think of going home to see his wife and his child, from whom he had been separated for three and a half years.

The day of his departure N'Tchambi, a poor lunatic who had been taken care of for a long time, wept like a child. "Doctor, have you told them not to send me away from here while you are gone?" The Doctor comforted him: "N'Tchambi, no one is allowed to send you away—otherwise he would get a terrible palaver from me!"

Sure enough, when the doctor came back, years later, there was N'Tchambi, weeping with joy. And he remained in the hospital for many more years—cared for to the moment when he died of his incurable illness.

Schweitzer's second homecoming to Europe was again darkened by sorrow. This time his beloved father had passed away, the man who had been closest to him all his life. The parsonage of Gunsbach, the home so dear to his memories, had to be turned over to the new minister.

He had spent only a short time with his wife and his little daughter when "S O S" letters started arriving from Lambaréné. They brought bad news: a new famine had broken out and another bad epidemic of dysentery. More doctors and nurses were urgently needed, more medical and surgical supplies were necessary.

Nothing could be done without money; Schweitzer had to find it. He made his plans and immediately began an extensive lecture tour of Europe. He talked about his hospital and the problems of Africa. In churches and in universities he explained what he meant by reverence for life: religious beliefs must be proved by action.

His words, his luminous face, his modesty, and his heart-warming sense of humor all combined to move everyone in his audience. And more and more people decided to show this wonderful man that they understood his words and wanted to help him in his work in far-off Africa, because he had awakened their conscience.

But "the Doctor who cured old Negroes in Africa" was also reputed to be able to cure old organs in Europe. And wherever he went Schweitzer was called to examine the organ and, of course, also to play it. Sometimes he was so tired that he asked to be awakened an hour before the concert started. To make up for the sleepless nights, during which he worked, he had fallen into the habit of sleeping in installments. Whenever he had a free moment, no matter where or when, he would take a nap to refresh himself.

Thanks to his unceasing efforts, he raised funds for Lambaréné. It would have been much easier to write letters begging for money for a good cause, or to sell charity stamps or booklets. But Albert Schweitzer's aim was much more than simple fund raising. He wanted to convince people that for the sake of their own consciences they should help others. He tried to open their minds, so that they could open their hearts.

The magic of his personality worked miracles. From every country of Europe gifts of every description began to arrive: boxes filled with medicines, surgical instruments, linen, canned food, evaporated milk.

To store all these gifts before they could be sent to Africa, Schweitzer rented a few modest rooms in an ancient house, 3 Rue des Greniers, in Strasbourg. Thirty years later he still stayed there whenever he came to Strasbourg. It became his last stop before returning to Africa. Here, under his close supervision and with his active help, every single item was carefully labeled and placed in a linen bag. These white linen bags were the only protection against the African ants.

Grateful as he was for the generous gifts of the wealthy, Schweitzer's greatest joy was in the small gifts which came from poor donors. Was it not wonderful? A hard-working laundress sent each week half a day's earning to help the hospital. The young inmates of a children's home decided to eat only soup once a month in order to provide money for an extra fish ration for the children of Lambaréné. Men and women of all classes offered part-time work for the benefit of their African brothers. Loads of letters came from people who had been moved by Schweitzer's example and who thanked him for showing them a way to help others.

With his amazing capacity for splitting his personality to become a doctor, a preacher, a musician, a philosopher, and a writer, Schweitzer was also one of the greatest experts on Goethe, the famous German poet. In the summer of 1928 he delivered an address on Goethe in Frankfort and was awarded the distinguished "Goethe Prize." With the money he received, he made a dream come true: he built his own little house in his beloved Gunsbach. Now he would have a permanent home in Europe, for himself and for the staff of his hospital. His roots then would continue to grow in the village of his childhood. It was the first time he had indulged in a personal luxury—the luxury of owning a home. He called it "the house that Goethe built."

12

World War II in the Jungle

When for the third time, in December, 1929, Schweitzer started on his long voyage to Africa, he was accompanied by his wife, by another doctor and two more nurses.

This time there were no bitter disappointments. Thanks to the devoted staff, the hospital was in good shape. With all the help, the *"Grand Docteur"*—the Great Doctor—was in ever greater demand. The natives all wanted to be treated by him. Even those who were not sick clamored for medicine. To get rid of these "imaginary" patients, Schweitzer had a special prescription: a few drops of bitter quinine in a glass of water—and the number of "sick" vanished like magic. Time was precious; it could not be wasted.

But when a man arrived at the hospital moaning, "Doctor, my head, oh, my head. I have such a terrible headache," Schweitzer would give him all his time. For this could be the symptom of the sleeping sickness in the first stage, and if it were so, there was the chance of a cure.

Laboratory work, operations—there were a hundred daily problems to be solved. Then the other Europeans could not stand the climate. After six or nine months, they sickened and had to be sent away to a more healthful spot until they recovered. Albert Schweitzer alone seemed to be immune to the tropical climate, with his healthy body disciplined by his powerful mind. "I have no time to be sick," he would say. But in his diaries he would note: "I am exhausted." Then he would go on to describe another African misery—toothache. Both Schweitzers suffered terribly, with not a single dentist within 300 miles! Schweitzer could make a temporary filling for his wife. But there was no one to help *him*. His feet, too, were badly infected at times, so that he could not walk and had to be carried from his house to the hospital. Yet there is scarcely a mention of all these and other painful moments in his diary.

Although he was still as busy as ever at the hospital and on its grounds during the day, thanks to the new staff, he now found free moments, especially at night, to concentrate on his writing. Publishers were waiting for his autobiography, for a third volume of the "History of Civilization" and for "The Mysticism of Paul the Apostle." Incredible as it may sound, he managed in his spare time to finish them all—a task which would have been a full-time job for every other writer.

In 1932, a letter came from the University of

the great city of Frankfort, Germany, inviting him to deliver an address on the 100th anniversary of the death of Goethe. Schweitzer accepted and sailed back to Europe.

Then, from 1934 to 1939, Schweitzer shuttled between Africa and Europe, switching from medical and missionary work in the jungle to philosophy and music in Europe. Translations of his books continued to appear in many languages. All the great universities invited him to give lectures. Churches pressed him for organ recitals. His fame grew.

In January, 1939, for the sixth time in five years, he was again en route to Europe, where he intended to work on his books. He had hardly set foot on French soil when he realized that war was on the point of breaking out. He had long anxiously followed the rise to power of Hitler, whom he considered a threat to humanity and to world peace. He now heard Hitler's roaring voice over the radio—war was unavoidable; it was imminent.

As usual, Schweitzer made up his mind immediately. His place was in Africa; his hospital needed him. He must not take the risk of being cut off from Lambaréné. He left his wife and his daughter, Rhena, in Switzerland—a traditionally neutral country—where they would be safe. Then he took the next boat back to Africa.

This time Albert Schweitzer remained in the jungle for nine long years, devoting himself entirely to the care of the sick. These were particularly difficult years, and without the gifts from America they would have been harder still. From this time dates Albert Schweitzer's profound gratitude to the American people.

Ships were being chased by German submarines, and one which was carrying drugs and surgical instruments was sunk by torpedoes. While Lambaréné was cut off from Europe, the hospital functioned thanks to American generosity. Although Schweitzer's name was not yet familiar to most Americans, philosophers, musicians, and missionaries knew of his work. It was they who spurred the creation of "Albert Schweitzer Societies," which in turn sent to Africa the urgently needed funds and supplies.

Schweitzer in the meantime had not been waiting for outside help. Somehow he and his hospital must survive, and to do this the hospital must become self-sufficient. Like a jack of all trades, Schweitzer built, farmed, dug ditches. Every bit of scrap was put to use. There was very rarely time now to work on his books or to play the piano-organ. But Schweitzer kept his hospital going and growing.

His greatest reward was to see that his example bore fruit; that his teachings were accepted by an ever-increasing number of natives. There was particularly one wonderful man, called Ojembo (which means "the song"). He taught in the boys' mission school and served as Schweitzer's interpreter at the Sunday preachings. Schweitzer described this native teacher as one of the finest men he had ever met. Ojembo was not much of a talker, but in a quiet way he absorbed every word Schweitzer said. Later he was transferred to another village and Schweitzer was disappointed never to hear from him. But to his deep happiness he learned, years later, that by adopting modern methods,

Ojembo had become a wealthy lumberman. With his money he had created a model village which, thanks to its plantations, was self-sufficient. It had the best school around, with classes for both children and adults. And, building entirely upon Schweitzer's teachings, Ojembo had created a true community.

Albert Schweitzer had a great gift for celebrating holidays, birthdays, and all kinds of special occasions. For the whole community such festive days were a most welcome interruption from the daily work and worries.

Of course, in the jungle one could not go out and buy gifts. But the smallest present—a raisin cake or an egg—was a rare luxury and a wonderful birthday gift. Whenever a new building was completed or a difficult irrigation work done, some kind of celebration followed.

Then there were the great holidays: Christmas, Easter, Whitsun. On such days the Doctor assembled his flock and preached. To make the Bible understandable to the natives, Albert Schweitzer changed certain words, always keeping close to the original meaning. For instance, instead of bread, he spoke of manioc; a horse was changed into an elephant, a cow into a goat, a field of wheat to a field of corn. He prepared his sermons with the greatest care, endeavoring to make religion truly comprehensible to the natives. He gave them the essence of the Christian religion, and illustrated it with pictures of their own world. His teachings of Jesus were adapted to their special mentality. Thus, slowly and gradually, the Doctor opened a window to a greater world of understanding.

One day a fine big church bell arrived at the hospital as a gift from France. Schweitzer consecrated it in a solemn ceremony. First he explained to the natives the meaning of a church bell. He told them it would sound from now on every Sunday and every weekday at nightfall. The natives listened attentively and one said, "Now we have understood. The bell is the voice of God, who calls for prayer on Sunday and for sleep at night. But the gong is the voice of the Doctor who calls for work!"

Small local events were also an occasion for festivity. For example, when the Doctor's tame chimpanzee got its new cage, he was carried in a gay procession to his lodgings, decorated with ripe bananas.

Picnics were a most popular kind of feast. When the sick had been cared for and the morning work was done, boxes with food were packed into the big canoe and a happy crowd went for an enjoyable outing. The air on the river was cool, and there was a lot to see on the way. After the meal on a sand bank, some stretched in the shade, others went exploring. Sometimes a baby crocodile was found and caught, or turtle eggs. Photographs were taken with a little camera which much impressed the natives. On the way home, they would tie up at a coffee plantation or stop to talk with the natives of a village and learn who was coming to the hospital.

On New Year's Eve the Doctor usually gave a little speech to his devoted co-workers and said a few words to the natives. On one occasion he said to them: "Thank you for being just what you are—for making me so happy—for often making me so mad . . . !"

In 1941, the Doctor received the happy surprise of his wife's arrival. With tremendous energy she had succeeded in making her long way through all the countries at war in order to join her husband. She knew there were no nurses to be had at this time, so she became a nurse again as she had been on that first arrival in Lambaréné almost thirty years before.

In 1945 when World War II was over, it still took a long time till adequate personnel for the hospital could be made available. It was October, 1948, when the Schweitzers could finally go back to visit with their daughter, who had been married to a Swiss organ builder, and to see their four grandchildren for the first time!

13

Schweitzer in America

The following summer, in July, 1949, Albert Schweitzer made his first trip to America.

Aboard the ship no one knew the nice white-haired gentleman who spent most of his time writing in his cabin. But when the young people in the tourist class wanted to dance, he was always ready to play the piano. And how well he played! Everybody liked this Dr. Schweitzer.

But on arriving in New York, great was their astonishment when a reception committee and a crowd of newspapermen surrounded their fellow-passenger and bombarded him with questions. None had suspected that this was such a famous man.

Schweitzer took America by storm. His picture was in all the newspapers—a giant with a thick mustache and unruly hair.

"When you see someone who looks like a Scotch terrier, it is me," Schweitzer had once written to a person whom he was to meet.

He came ashore wearing an old-fashioned black coat, a stiff collar, and a weatherbeaten hat. He was delighted with everything he saw.

Photographers shot pictures, and Schweitzer answered every question they asked. "Without American help, my hospital would never have survived the war," and he would forever remain grateful for what they had done, he said.

His friendliness, his sense of humor, and his incredible simplicity made an overwhelming impression. This was the stuff heroes were made of—Americans loved it.

Friends took Albert Schweitzer for a sight-seeing tour of New York. They showed him the superlative achievements of the Big Town. "But then," Schweitzer recalled, "when we passed over the great George Washington Bridge, I saw my friend hastily searching his pockets. There in the biggest city of the world, with all the technical miracles, I saw that good old-fashioned institution of the Middle Ages: the bridge toll! In the Middle Ages the robber barons exacted a toll from the wayfarers—today it is the car drivers." And he chuckled with pleasure!

Schweitzer had come to America on invitation to give the key speech at the 200th anniversary of Geothe's birth, which was to be celebrated at Aspen, Colorado. On his way to Colorado, Schweitzer visited Boston and Chicago, where the latter University gave him an honorary degree. He was welcomed everywhere with enthusiasm. A young American newspaperman accompanied him. It took him a while to learn the ways of the famous man.

Albert Schweitzer always carried his own

suitcase—it was no use trying to take it from him. And wherever he saw a woman carrying a heavy burden, he ran after her. He would carry her suitcase. This put the young American in an awkward position and obliged him to run after other women, to help them!

The reason why Schweitzer acted this way was that years before, when he and his wife had been prisoners of war in France, they once had to pack their belongings in great haste to catch a train. They could hardly move under the heavy load. A cripple, whom Schweitzer had treated in the prison, offered his help. It was more than welcome. This act so moved Schweitzer that he made a vow: He would give a hand to anyone, anywhere, in the same predicament. As with all his vows, he kept this one all his life.

Wherever he traveled, he produced the same reaction. The sight of old Dr. Schweitzer carrying other people's suitcases always induced younger people, who may not have given it a thought, to do the same.

Aspen, which lies at an altitude of some eight

thousand feet in the Rocky Mountains, proved strenuous for Albert Schweitzer. So he stayed only a few days. Even this brief visit made an unforgettable impression. His speech on Goethe was magnificent. He delivered it in two languages, French and German. Thornton Wilder translated it, sentence by sentence, into English.

The audience was enthralled. Others before and after him talked about Goethe. Learned scholars from all the countries of the world had come to speak at Aspen. But Schweitzer spoke in simple words to describe the greatness of the genius of Goethe. This simplicity, of course, was the result of painstaking preparation. Schweitzer had worked on his address for three months and, as usual, had rewritten it several times.

More than his words, the sight of his luminous personality and the knowledge of his accomplishments impressed everyone immensely. All wanted to know more about him and his hospital. All wanted to read his books. And of course everyone wanted to talk to him.

Particularly the young people. It was the first time they had met a man who had made an adventure of spiritual life. Every word he said seemed to make sense. They never had enough of his stories about life in the jungle and about his experiences with both men and beasts. Also Schweitzer had a great respect for young people; he understood them, talked their language. He exhorted them to stand by their ideals and never to forsake them just because someone said that "one had to be realistic when one grew up."

"If only adults had the idealism of the fourteen-year-old, the world would be a better place to live in," he said. "The power of idealism is incalculable. We see no power in a drop of water. But let it get into a crack in the rock and be turned to ice and it splits the rock. Turned into steam, it drives the pistons of the most powerful engines."

Young and old were fascinated by this man who radiated kindness and simplicity. Wherever he went—to play the organ in a church, to make a speech, to pay a visit to friends—he charmed one and all.

Schweitzer stayed in America only a short time and yet the results of his visit were enormous. Worshiped, admired for many years by groups of Europeans, he was known to comparatively few, and considered more or less a legend by many. It was his trip to America which started Albert Schweitzer on his road to world fame.

"Reverence for life" appealed to Americans, to their sense of decency, to their community spirit. Here was Christianity in action. And here, too, was an example of what one man could achieve when equipped with faith, courage and good will. Albert Schweitzer embodied the American pioneer spirit.

14

Fame Comes to the Hospital

Schweitzer now had two established homes: his jungle hospital in Lambaréné and his little house in Gunsbach. The two worlds were as different from each other as they could be: the one, tropical, peopled with dark-skinned Africans, with lepers and with wild animals; the other, a cheerful Alsatian village, surrounded by vineyards and orchards, peopled with sturdy

villagers, who spoke the dialect of his childhood.

His family and his friends pleaded with Albert Schweitzer to come back and to settle in
his native country. Had he not earned a well-
deserved rest? "You cannot burn a candle at
both ends," they said. "Yes," Schweitzer smil-
ingly replied, stretching himself to his six-foot
height, "you can, if the candle is long enough!"

And at the end of every three months' vacation in Europe, he returned to his African head-
quarters as before. The only difference was that
now his medical supplies increased with every
trip. Thanks to his fame, gifts from all sides
accumulated in the storehouse. And he called at
all the great laboratories, keen on bringing
home to Lambaréné the latest discoveries in the
field of tropical medicine.

Every time he left Gunsbach for Africa, he
spent a week at the storage house in Strasbourg.
Clad in a white apron, he not only supervised
the packing of the hundreds of trunks, he also
carefully labeled most of them himself. Old
friends came in and went out, lending a hand

and chatting with the Doctor, who was always ready for a laugh between chores. Usually, toward the end of November he was ready to leave.

The amount of mail which he carried, with the intention of reading and answering on the long sea voyage, was enormous. Once it filled four large potato bags. The customs officer at Bordeaux asked, "What have you there?" "Letters," Schweitzer answered. The customs officer was not going to let this man make a fool of him. He ordered Schweitzer to open the sacks. He searched them thoroughly for hidden merchandise and found—nothing but letters. Grudgingly he gave up.

Lambaréné had become famous. The hospital now was nothing like the old hen house in which Albert Schweitzer had started to practice! It was an impressive settlement: 45 buildings, barracks, small and large houses, storage buildings, surrounded by vegetable gardens, coffee and cocoa plantations and orchards.

These orchards were Schweitzer's special joy and pride. He had planned them from the beginning. "We will make a Garden of Eden around the hospital, with so many fruit trees, papayas, oranges, pineapples, that there will no longer be such crime as stealing!"

Devoted physicians were doing medical and surgical work under Schweitzer's supervision. There were the splendid nurses who, for thirty years, had shared all the Doctor's problems: Mathilde Kottmann and Emma Hausknecht. There was also young Ali Silver, a sweet-faced Dutch girl, who took care of the lepers. These women had renounced everything and given their lives to help Schweitzer in Africa.

Numerous visitors now arrived by plane at the nearby airport of Brazzaville. They often showed surprise at the sight of the primitive installations. Now that he had adequate funds, they asked, why did not Albert Schweitzer build a modern hospital with the latest technical equipment?

Many visitors were frankly disillusioned.

They wondered why the Doctor failed to provide the Negroes with all the facilities which were to be found in an up-to-date hospital. The answer was very simple: Schweitzer wanted them healthy *his* way—but he wanted them happy *their* way.

No, this was not a hospital in our sense of the word, nor even a quiet home for the sick. Here you heard the laughter and shouts of men, women, and children. The place was filled with noise and various activities. Fires were gaily burning. Here linen was washed. There a group of mothers were feeding their babies at their breasts. A woman lovingly searched a little bushy head for lice. It was an African hospital, a happy community.

The natives believed that it brought luck to name a baby after a powerful person, to keep the evil spirits away. They christened it with the full name—titles and all. In time there were quite a number of little black *Doctor Albert Schweitzers* running through the jungle. And in native villages many a little girl was called *Mademoiselle Emma* or *Mademoiselle Ma-*

thilde, after the nurses of the Lambaréné hospital.

With every passing year there was less ignorance, more community spirit and, most important of all—ever fewer sicknesses. Thanks to the latest discoveries, there was even new hope for the most miserable of the sick, the lepers. This was what counted, and this was why Albert Schweitzer continued his work with the same indestructible enthusiasm.

He did not care to impress foreign visitors with a model hospital, which would not answer the jungle needs. But the sight of the fabulous Doctor climbing up a ladder to repair the roof never failed to make an impression. To see the octogenarian swinging an axe, lending a hand everywhere, and directing every kind of work with that professional touch he had acquired during his hardest years—these sights left no onlooker untouched.

And late at night, after a day so busy that every visitor was exhausted, they marveled at the Doctor who sat at the piano to play for their and his own enjoyment. Music transfigured him;

it smoothed the wrinkles of his furrowed face. And the hands which had worked so hard all through the day now transmitted with sensitive fingers the sounds of Bach's or Mozart's symphonies.

15

Schweitzer in Gunsbach

When the news spread that Dr. Schweitzer was back from Africa, his native village turned into a place of pilgrimage. From all over Europe, from America, from Asia came people who wanted to see with their own eyes one of the greatest men of their time. The magic of his name became such that some even believed only he could lead them to a happier life.

Schweitzer's home was a simple, small, three-story house which stood on the main street. His room was on the ground floor. Furnished like a monk's cell, it had an iron bed, a table, two chairs. On two big nails on the wall hung Schweitzer's black Loden cape and his wide-brimmed hat. A few photographs and ebony carvings, gifts from Negroes, were the only decorations. This was the room where he slept and where he wrote whenever he had any time during the day. His work table stood by the window, so he could take part in the life of the village. He loved to look out, recognize a friend passing through the street and get up from his chair for a little chat. He knew everybody here by name, for all were friends of his youth or the children, or the grandchildren—with time also the great grandchildren—of those he had known as a boy.

To the villagers, famous Dr. Schweitzer was simply *Monsieur Albert*. They loved him; they were proud of him; but they also respected his privacy. Nobody ever bothered him with pleas for his autograph or for his picture. He was simply one of them. To show him their affection, they made many touching little gestures: for instance, not a day would pass without someone placing on his window sill a few fine apples, or a big bunch of grapes, or perhaps some fresh walnuts.

A day in Gunsbach was just as full as an African day. But here, instead of practicing medicine, he practiced music. Early in the morning, he played the piano for two hours. After breakfast he did some writing. At eleven o'clock he invariably walked over to the church.

The church dominated the little community of Gunsbach. Situated on a small hill, its white tower topped with the weather cock could be seen from every spot in the valley. Inside, the church was very modest. It had plain wooden benches, poor lighting, and a big stovepipe that cut clear across the interior. Except for a statue of Christ and some quotations from the Bible, the walls were bare. But it had a peculiar charm; its warm, homely atmosphere was felt by all who entered it. Gunsbach families had worshiped here for generations and had left their imprint on this church, which was a part of their sturdy, laborious lives.

Albert Schweitzer climbed up the steep, narrow steps of the little wooden staircase which led up to the loft where the organ stood. He climbed them as nimbly and happily as when he was a little boy, and as thankfully as ever.

Then he took off his shoes, changing them for what he called his "ballet slippers." These were soft, comfortable shoes, perfect for pushing the pedals. And then he played and he played—oblivious to all that went on around him.

He rehearsed some difficult passage in Bach until he was satisfied that he had mastered it. Or he played a fugue from one end to another.

He seldom was alone in the church. For always some friends or visitors begged to hear him. "You are going to be terribly bored," he warned them, "you will hear me repeating the same thing over and over again!" But they came, nevertheless, and no one would ever forget the experience.

Albert Schweitzer had played on the finest organs of the great cathedrals of the world. But to him the little organ of his village church, which he had designed, seemed the best of all. He lovingly called it his "Arabian horse."

The Gunsbach organ, built according to the oldest traditions, represented a minimum of mechanical work. It was the last word in simplicity.

To make recordings of Schweitzer playing Bach on this Gunsbach organ was a wonderful idea, but not an easy one to realize. In the summer of 1951, a group of young Americans decided to try.

They brought with them a large American sound truck, equipped with the newest, most perfect instruments for recording music. It even had its own power generator placed on a trailer.

It took the Americans considerable time to persuade Albert Schweitzer to make these re-

cordings. What convinced him was the assur-
ance that he would hear himself playing as soon
as the recording was made. If there were anything he wanted to correct, they would erase it.
He could then play the passage again, which
they would record and play back once more for
his approval. Once convinced, Schweitzer as
usual translated his enthusiasm into a frenzy
of work.

Had it been a contraption from the planet
Mars, it would not have seemed more out of
place than this modern magic from the U.S.A.
Standing against a background of fifteenth-cen-
tury houses which faced the old church, it had
on one side a pigsty with a heap of manure, on
the other an open well.

During the recording sessions, all kinds of
appliances had to be installed in the church.
The technicians were afraid of disturbing Albert Schweitzer with their comings and goings.
But Schweitzer, with a lock of his hair falling
over his face, went on playing on his organ as if
they did not exist.

The arrival of those four Americans with their sound truck attracted no end of foreign visitors, famous musicians, organists, conductors. They mixed with the villagers, filling the pews during the long hours Albert Schweitzer was playing.

Typically, Schweitzer would not interfere with the schedule of the workers who were busy repairing the church tower, badly damaged during the war. They had to go on working till 5 P.M. He would play when they were through.

The temperature in the church was kept low because heat would have harmed the organ. But if some of the shivering listeners were aware of it—it happened to be a rainy, stormy summer—Albert Schweitzer never felt the cold. Such discomfort simply did not exist for him.

Following each recording, he came down the steps and out to the truck to listen to the playback. Many a time a single passage of Bach was recorded again and again until it met with his approval.

Thanks to this devoted teamwork between

America and Gunsbach, millions of people are now able to listen to the recorded playing of Albert Schweitzer on his favorite organ.

16

Honors and Hardships

In his Gunsbach village the great old man had little privacy; he was a victim of his international fame.

A cross section of humanity stopped at his house; the little and the great followed each other: cardinals, politicians, musicians, physicians, the Queen Mother of Belgium, painters, sculptors, shopkeepers, farmers, ministers, students. Every mail brought hundreds of letters, every other one of them a call from a person in distress.

The little house became a beehive. The devoted household staff was busy coping with the Herculean task of taking care of a man who wanted to take care of the whole world with the exception of himself. They struggled hard to conform with his strict orders never to turn away anyone who wanted to see him. At the same time they did their best to keep free a few scattered half hours for his rest and privacy.

There was no use trying to deceive him. A visitor would be told that the Doctor was not at home or too busy to receive him. From his ground floor room, Albert Schweitzer saw all and heard all through his open door. Much to the dismay of his faithful guards, he would make a sudden appearance and welcome the almost-disposed-of visitor.

There was always open house, and hospitality was warmly offered to all comers. The keeper of the Gunsbach home and closest co-worker of the Doctor for nearly forty years was wonderful Madame Emmy Martin. Every day she was ready to provide substantial meals for an unpredictable number of visitors.

Albert Schweitzer usually ate with his ailing wife in her room or was served on a tray in his own room. His meals were frugal: some fruit, nuts, and cereals. But he never failed to join his guests in the small dining room before they had finished their meal. In a relaxed mood, he sat down to talk. No matter what the profession or nationality of the guests, he always found a story that fitted the occasion. His incredible memory helped him record incidents and experiences with the innumerable people he had met in his long life. As for topics, he was never at a loss. There was hardly a trade or a job he had not tackled himself in Africa, or that did not interest him.

One morning a carpet dealer touring the country in his station wagon stopped at the Gunsbach house. He did not know who lived there. Albert Schweitzer opened the door and, much to his amusement, was offered carpets for sale. He gently explained to the salesman that he had no use for his carpets. But then he started to discuss carpets with great interest. He gave the salesman such sound professional advice on how to clean them that the dealer asked, "Has Monsieur been in the business?" He became speechless when he discovered that he had been talking to the great Dr. Albert Schweitzer.

Schweitzer was literally besieged with requests for pictures by every visitor equipped with a camera, and of course by reporters sent by their newspapers. While visibly annoyed with the never-ending requests of the visitors, Dr. Schweitzer was incredibly kind and patient with the staff photographers, although posing was always a great strain. He believed that famous people were usually too ungracious to photographers. "They are here to do their job; they come to me because they have been assigned to do it, not for their own pleasure nor for mine. So I have to coöperate with them. Why make life miserable for these nice fellows who are doing such a difficult job?"

Patiently he took any pose indicated by the

photographers, as long as it was a natural one. "You want me to sit—to stand—to walk? All right!" But the moment the delighted photographers asked Schweitzer to pretend he was talking to someone, or to make the slightest gesture that was against his nature, he was unrelenting. "I never pretend to do a thing. Tell me how you want to shoot me, but never ask me to pretend."

Schweitzer, needless to say, was an ideal model for painters and sculptors. Because of his thick hair and his bushy mustache, it seems that sculptures of Albert Schweitzer sometimes resembled the head of Joseph Stalin. As a result, one day, the kind Doctor's likeness was stoned by outraged anti-communists who had taken it for Stalin's. The story greatly amused Schweitzer.

Albert Schweitzer always led an ascetic life. He suffered at the very idea of a single superfluous cent being wasted on himself. He was generous with others and he never had enough for his jungle hospital. With its six hundred fami-

MONON PUBLIC LIBRARY

lies depending entirely on him for housing, feeding, and medical care, he needed a great deal of money. But for himself he needed very little.

He did all his traveling third-class, which on a long trip in Europe could mean sitting for several nights on a wooden bench. When asked by a worried friend why, he answered: "I travel third-class because there is no fourth-class any more!"

His sense of thrift was such that he would never write a personal letter on a clean sheet of paper. The back side of printed matter or any old scrap of paper was fine for this purpose.

He simply hated to see anything wasted and had a truly ingenious way of finding use for seemingly useless things—tin covers, old cardboard boxes, string, odds and ends of all kinds. He always had in mind how precious the most insignificant item would have been in the jungle.

His wardrobe was famous for its longevity. He wore his shoes to the very end. His black Loden cape and his crumpled hat served him for at least thirty years. His white linen jackets were always neat, though threadbare and mended. And there was that spectacular black suit he had worn on every great occasion of his long and illustrious life. The suit was made for him in 1915 by his friend and contemporary, the village tailor of Gunsbach, Mr. Stoehr. Both the proud tailor and the modest Dr. Schweitzer saw no reason why this suit was not good enough for the finest occasions!

Before taking his daily walk to the church or an evening stroll along the road, Albert Schweitzer went to the kitchen to gather bones and meat leftovers. With this loot he made the rounds of the dogs of the neighborhood, enjoying their pleasure in an extra ration. He would stop every farmer who chanced along the road to pet the horse and inquire about its health. He could not suffer the sight of a man remaining in his seat while the horse pulled the cart up a steep hill. "You must step down," he would say, "and gently talk to your horse when the road is steep!"

Schweitzer loved animals in his old age as much as when he was a little boy and had included them in his daily prayers. And he spoke out whenever he saw cruelty or carelessness.

Schweitzer's devotion to animals proved quite dramatic on a very special occasion.

In 1952 Albert Schweitzer received the greatest honor France bestows on her great men. He was elected to become a member of the "Académie Française."

The French Academy, part of "L'Institut de France," was founded in 1635 by Cardinal Richelieu to honor the most distinguished men of France in the fields of literature, morals and science. The members were called "The Immortals." There were forty seats for writers and poets, forty for scientists. When one of them died, a successor was chosen to occupy his seat. The seating was celebrated with the greatest pomp, according to the old tradition.

Republican guards on horseback paraded in front of the Academy and the venerable members filed in one by one, clad in magnificently embroidered green tailcoats and feathered hats.

Schweitzer, of course, walked in wearing his famous old black suit made by Mr. Stoehr.

Every new member had to deliver a long speech, which was later published and considered a classic. Albert Schweitzer had worked on his speech for months. He was to talk about the "Evolution of Ethics."

The day he arrived in Paris to become an "immortal," he bought a newspaper. Big headlines proclaimed: "Guests of the President of the Republic Go Hunting. Prince of the Netherlands Wins First Honors: Kills 145 Pieces of Game!"

Schweitzer was outraged. How could the barbaric custom of hunting with pack hounds be glorified as a heroic action!

When he delivered his speech before the illustrious assembly, he added one paragraph about the inhumanity of hunting. He cared not at all that this criticism was directed at the President of France and the members of royal families. It seemed much more important to him to speak out for the cause of the animals.

After the seating ceremony, while the high dignitaries and members of the Academy celebrated with festive dinner parties, Albert Schweitzer invited a few close friends to a little old Parisian restaurant, Café Voltaire. Half a century before he had often taken his meals here. "It is the place where my little daughter ordered dinner herself for the first time and gave the first tip herself!" he recalled.

The food here was very poor, but Schweitzer gently insisted that everything should be eaten in order not to hurt the feelings of the owner. Food was not what the guests had come for. Schweitzer in his gayest mood made a feast of the evening.

In 1952 Albert Schweitzer was awarded the Nobel Prize for peace. This prize had been instituted by Alfred Nobel, a wealthy Swede, inventor, and industrialist, who died in 1896. He had made his fame and fortune with dynamite. Dynamite was a dreadful killer, so dreadful that many thought at the time it would put an end to war. Surely, no nation would dare use it. But they were wrong.

Having given the world this terrible weapon, Alfred Nobel then tried to find an incentive for scientists to work for peace and to pursue research for the sake of pure knowledge. He left his money to be distributed every year to the most deserving men throughout the world in the literary, scientific, and philanthropic fields.

When the Peace Prize was awarded to Albert Schweitzer, he was in Africa. With him was a nephew, who was the first to hear the great news over the radio. Even though it was late at night, he rushed into his uncle's room and without any explanation enthusiastically congratulated him. Schweitzer grinned: "So finally it has happened. My black cat has had her kittens! That is splendid!" It was the best news he could think of at that moment.

The next morning, while headlines in the world's papers told about the winner of the Nobel Prize for peace, the recipient was helping to clean out the antelopes' pen at Lambaréné. It had to be done every three or four months and it was quite a job. The dung was most precious as manure, but the antelopes did not like the intrusion and got very nervous. That was why Schweitzer would not let the natives do it alone. His job was to gather the seven or eight antelopes around him and talk to them soothingly while the enclosure was cleaned out.

But Schweitzer's happiness about the prize showed itself in many little ways. Out for a walk with Tsu-Tsu, his pet dog, Schweitzer would say, "You must stop hunting now! We have received the Nobel Prize for peace; you are a Nobel dog. If you don't behave, they will take the money back, and you know very well how we need it for our lepers; so you better behave!"

It was the custom for Nobel Prize winners to travel to Norway for the solemn ceremony. An exception was made for Albert Schweitzer, the 77-year-old Doctor who was too busy working in his jungle hospital to make a special trip to Norway. He asked permission to postpone the ceremony to another year, when he was planning to be in Europe.

In November, 1954, once more the "good black suit" came out of moth balls. Attired in his stiff collar and black bow tie, Schweitzer received the Nobel Prize in Oslo from the hands of King Haakon of Norway.

Following the distribution of the prizes, he delivered a wonderful speech on a very serious note. He spoke about the problems of men in the Atomic Age—how superhuman inventions made man inhuman. He pleaded for a renewal of spiritual values. He spoke standing erect for nearly an hour, no mean feat for a man of his age, and his every word was a clear appeal to the conscience of the world.

The Nobel Prize not only brought the Doctor the great honor he deserved, but also a fine sum of money. What a blessing for the hospital, which of course received all of it. At last, Schweitzer could fulfill his dream of building a village for lepers. While separated from the rest of the community, here they could live more pleasantly and in greater comfort than before.

Honors and awards followed one another in quick and splendid succession. There was hardly a great university which had not given the fabulous Doctor an honorary degree.

In 1955 Albert Schweitzer was invited to London, where, in Buckingham Palace, Queen Elizabeth invested him with the insignia of the "Order of Merit." This was one of the most coveted orders bestowed by the Crown. Only 24 living Britons may hold it at any time. The only other non-Briton honored with this medal was President Eisenhower.

In London Schweitzer did not want to stay in a hotel. He chose to receive all his distinguished visitors in a cozy little tearoom whose owner was an old Alsatian friend.

The English, who had always loved and admired Albert Schweitzer, were delighted to have him with them. Once, as he walked through the streets, someone stopped him, tapped him on the shoulder, and said, "Old

man, you have worked well!" With a mischie-
vous smile, Schweitzer turned to his companion
and commented, "Nobody ever said this to me
when I was in school!"

17

Albert Schweitzer's Greatness

Fame and honors did not change Albert Schweitzer. He continues to live in the simplest manner among the African natives. Lambaréné has become more and more a home to him. Once, when quietly speaking of death, he said, "If I am called to God during one of my visits in Gunsbach, I want to lie beside my own people in the Gunsbach cemetery. But if I fall into my last sleep in Africa, then I want to be buried in Lambaréné. It is logical to lie where one falls, and the earth is God's earth, no matter where it is!"

His greatest hope is that the hospital will continue to develop after he is no longer there.

Albert Schweitzer is, of course, constantly asked questions about all the great problems of the day. He recognizes their gravity, but he refuses to comment on the "isms" which separate the world. He is convinced that mutual understanding is possible if, abandoning fear and prejudices, we turn back to the true values of life. "We have lost the great humane ideals," he said. "We have to find our way back to humanism."

"But, Doctor, how can we find this way?"

"It is so clear: by being kind and by being simple," he answers.

What is it that makes Albert Schweitzer one of the greatest men of his time?

His belief in deeds, not words. Albert Schweitzer practices what others only preach:

he has devoted himself to the service of his fellowmen.

His complete naturalness and sincerity. He has always been himself and he believes that all people should be themselves at all times.

His acceptance of hardships. Through the years, difficulties for him were a challenge. He overcame them by his faith and his will power.

His courage. He has had the courage to do what his conscience tells him, even under the most difficult circumstances.

His simplicity. The simplest man can understand his teachings. He says every word clearly. He appeals to the conscience, to the common sense, and to the heart of every man.

His optimism. Knowing of the sufferings and miseries of mankind, he has devoted himself to relieving them. Yet in his heart he remains an optimist.

His belief in the power of ideals. All over the world, young people take inspiration from Albert Schweitzer, not only from his words but especially from his acts. Yet it is not followers that Albert Schweitzer wants. He wants each person to find within himself the power to realize his own personal ideals.

His love for life and for all that lives. He has always done all he could to help others to love life and to feel reverence for all living things.

His faith that seeds of kindness can never be lost, as sun rays never are lost.

The wonderful adventure he has made of living his ideals.

Index

LANDMARK BOOKS

LANDMARK BOOKS *continued*

WORLD LANDMARK BOOKS

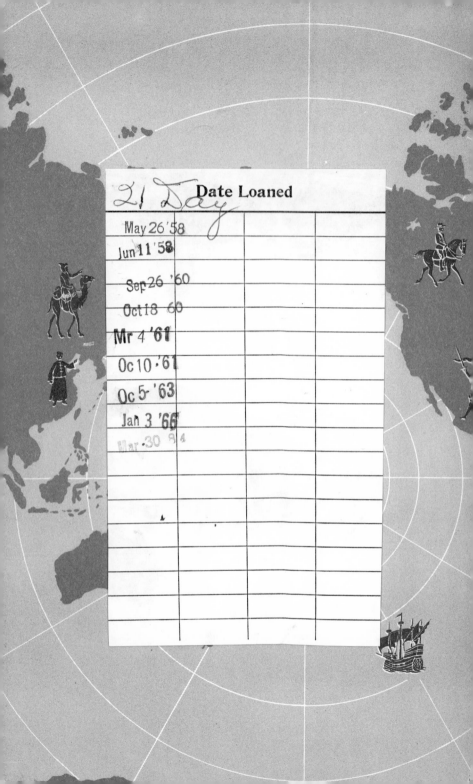

21 Day

Date Loaned

May 26 '58		
Jun 11 '58		
Sep 26 '60		
Oct 18 '60		
Mr 4 '61		
Oc 10 '61		
Oc 5 '63		
Jan 3 '66		
Mar 30 '84		